SUSHI FOR PARTIES
MAKI-ZUSHI AND NIGIRI-ZUSHI
Ken Kawasumi

Sushi is one of the truly Japanese dishes. It makes full use of fresh seafood and seasonal ingredients. A Japanese eating sushi exclaims that he or she is happy to be born Japanese. Along with sukiyaki and tempura, sushi is world famous as a typical Japanese dish. Traditionally, chirashi-zushi (scattered sushi) and maki-zushi (rolled sushi) have been prepared by mothers for the occasion of cherry-blossom viewing, school sports, festivals and traditional events. It is also served for guests. Like home-made pickles, each family had its own distinctive flavor.

The flavor of sushi has been handed down like this from generation to generation, but recently it has been forgotten with the increase in nuclear families. Nigiri-zushi in particular has become high-priced food available only at sushi bars.

This book is intended for beginners. TV champion Ken Kawasumi, who won the sushi contest sponsored by TV Tokyo twice, explains the techniques and methods simply and plainly. If nigiri-zushi is prepared at home, everyone can relish the intriguing recipes at a reasonable cost. Let's enjoy and fully appreciate the delicacies of hand-made sushi.

SUSHI FOR PARTIES

Maki-zushi and Nigiri-zushi
by Ken Kawasumi

Copyright ©1996 Graph-sha Ltd.
All rights reserved.

Published by Graph-sha Ltd., Tokyo, Japan
Translated by Kazuhiko Nagai

Distributed by
Japan Publications Trading Co., Ltd.,
P.O. Box 5030 Tokyo International,
Tokyo, Japan

Distributed in the United States by
Kodansha America, Inc., through
Oxford University Press, 198
Madison Avenue, New York, NY 10016

First edition, First printing: March 1996
Tenthprinting: September 2000

ISBN: 0-87040-956-5

☆   ☆   ☆

Metric Conversion Table:
    1 Tbsp (tablespoon) = 15 cc
    1 tsp (teaspoon) = 5 cc
    1 cup = 200 cc
  Sushi rice 1 cup = 180 cc

Sake and *mirin* are often used in Japanese
Cooking.
* *Sake* (rice wine) mellows food, tones down raw
  taste or smells and improves flavor.
  Dry sherry can be a substitute for *sake*.
* *Mirin* (sweet cooking rice wine) is used to
  improve flavor and give food glaze and sweet-
  ness. *Mirin* may be substituted with 1 Tbsp *sake*
  and 1 tsp sugar.
  Both *sake* and *mirin* are now manufactured in
  the USA.

About the author:

Ken Kawasumi was born in 1956 in Kamakura.
He started his apprenticeship at the age of 16 at famous
local sushi bars. He focused on improving his own
techniques and developed original maki-zushi.
He captured the championship twice at the All Japan
Professional Sushi Contest sponsored by TV Tokyo.
He also won a bronze medal at the All Japan Sushi
Technique Contest sponsored by the Japan Sushi
Association. He now runs a sushi bar, 'Kawasumi' and
teaches sushi at various schools.

Printed in Japan

Contents

A VARIETY OF ATTRACTIVE SUSHI

Colorful Sushi for the Four Seasons

Sushi Painting

SOUPS TO ACCOMPANY SUSHI

DISHES THAT GO WELL WITH SAKE

FANCY MAKI-ZUSHI
(Rolled Sushi)

Sushi rice is colored with oboro or powdered condiments and various patterns are designed by manipulation of the ingredients. It is an exciting moment when the finished rolled rice is cut as fantastic designs appear. Presented here are 17 maki-zushi, ranging from a traditional pine-bamboo-plum roll and a floating chrysanthemum roll to original panda and butterfly rolls.

BASIC SEASONED SUSHI RICE

Ingredients (for 2 lbs or 900 g):
3 cups (540 cc) rice
3 cups (540 cc) water
Vinegar mixture:
  5 Tbsp vinegar
  3⅓ Tbsp sugar
  1 Tbsp salt
  1 sheet of kombu
  [1¼″ (3 cm) square]

★ Use the same amount of rice and water. For new rice, decrease water by 10%, and for old rice increase water by 10%. For children, use less salt and vinegar.

1 Wash rice until water is clear. Measure the water and add to rice in a heavy pot. Set aside for 30 minutes. Bring to a boil. When cooked, turn off heat and allow to continue to steam for 20 minutes.

2 Prepare vinegar mixture by mixing ingredients in a pan over heat. Stop the heat just before it comes to a boil. Remove kombu.

3 Empty cooked rice into a dampened wooden flat bowl. Pour the vinegar mixture over the rice using a spatula to distribute it evenly as shown in the photo.

4 Separate rice starting from the outside making cutting motions and spread.

5 When rice is spread all over, gather together to one side.

6 Using the spatula diagonally, make cutting motions. Gather again and repeat the same.

7 While using a fan to aid cooling, turn the hot rice so that the vinegar solution is well absorbed. Repeat the same again.

8 Gather together in one place and cover with wet cloth. Let cool it until it reaches body temperature.

PREPARATIONS FOR FANCY MAKI-ZUSHI

MAKISU (Bamboo rolling mat)

There are two types of makisu: one is for making thick rolls and the other for making thin rolls. Choose a tightly woven makisu with the string ends on one side. Use with the right side up. After use, clean in water and dry thoroughly so as to avoid mold.

THE SIZE OF NORI (Laver seaweed)

The basic size used in this book is a sheet of nori cut in half. When an uncut sheet is used, it is referred to as 'a whole sheet of nori.' Place a piece of nori lengthwise and cut in half as shown in the photo below. When using an omelet sheet, cut the sheet the same size as the nori. When you get used to this method, try a whole sheet of nori.

Place the nori on a makisu with the glossy side down.

8¼″ (21 cm)

7″ (18 cm)

How to cut

1 sheet = 4⅛″ × 7″
          (10.5 × 18 cm)
½ sheet = 4⅛″ × 3½″
          (10.5 × 9 cm)
⅓ sheet = 4⅛″ × 2⅜″
          (10.5 × 6 cm)
¼ sheet = 4⅛″ × 1¾″
          (10.5 × 4.5 cm)

HOW TO ROLL

A Thin Roll
It is difficult to handle the makisu in the usual way, so roll the rice as if rubbing your hands.

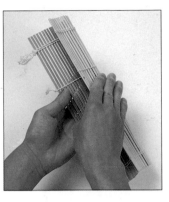

How to Add Rice
When adding rice, place the makisu on the palm of your hand, spread the rice and roll.

Two types of Rolling

When rolling the semicylindrical type, place the edge of nori or omelet sheet so that it comes to the underside and adjust by makisu. In the case of the cylindrical type, lift the makisu with both hands after rolled and adjust the shape by moving from side to side.

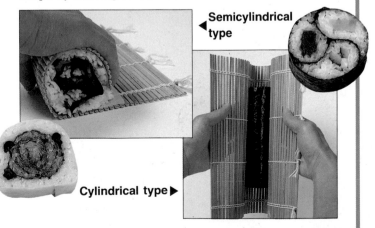

◄ Semicylindrical type

Cylindrical type ►

BARA-MAKI
(Rose Roll)

Ingredients (1 roll):
3 Tbsp oboro (p.25)
1 pickled green leaf stalk (13" / 33 cm)
1 oz (30 g) red pickled ginger
7 oz (200 g) sushi rice (p.6)
1 thin egg omelet
toasted nori

Preparations: Add oboro to 3½ oz (100 g) sushi rice and mix well. Cut pickled green leaf stalk into three. See page 51 for the thin egg sheet.

Put red sushi rice sparsely on 2 sheets of nori. Scatter chopped red ginger all over.

Join the 2 sheets of nori lengthwise and roll up from the front going away from you. This makes flowers.

Spread 3½ oz(100 g) sushi rice on the thin egg sheet leaving ⅜" (1 cm) above. Put three ⅜"(1 cm) sheets of nori and indent each with a chopstick.

Place green leaf stalks on each indentation. These make leaves.

Place the flower between the second and third green leaf stalks.

Roll up so that the joint of egg sheet comes to the underside. Shape the roll with makisu in a semicylindrical form.

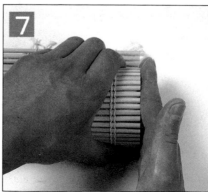

Move the roll on the one side and flatten. Moisten a sharp knife and cut the roll into four equal parts.

TULIP-MAKI
(Tulip Roll)

Ingredients (1 roll):
4¼" (11 cm) cucumber (Japanese variety or similar size is best)
4¼"(11 cm) pickled green leaves

red pickled ginger
toasted white sesame seeds
8 oz (230 g) sushi rice (p.6)
toasted nori

Preparations: Select a straight cucumber. For Japanese cucumbers cut in half lengthwise. For larger cucumbers cut slices approximately 1¼"(3 cm) leaving peel intact. Use inside of cucumber for other dishes.

Join 1 sheet plus ¼ sheet nori (4⅛" × 8¾", 10.5 × 22.5 cm) and spread 4¼ oz(120 g) sushi rice over them leaving ¾" (2 cm) spaces on top and bottom. Make two mounds 1¼" (3 cm) high in the center with 1 oz (30 g) each of sushi rice.

Close the nori on the inside of mounds and make a stalk. Attach cucumbers to the nori on the outside of mounds.

Sprinkle sesame seeds on both sides of the mounds. Place ½ sheet of nori between the mounds and press down with a chopstick.

Put red ginger and pickled green leaves in this order in the hollow groove in the center. The red ginger makes a flower and green leaves a calyx.

Put the makisu on the palm and make a slight curve. Stuff ⅓ oz (10 g) each of sushi rice between cucumbers and rice.

Put 1 oz (30 g) of sushi rice on all and cover the nori and cucumbers.

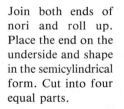

Join both ends of nori and roll up. Place the end on the underside and shape in the semicylindrical form. Cut into four equal parts.

TOMBO-MAKI
(Dragonfly Roll)

Ingredients (1 roll):
8¾″ (22 cm) pokeweed (a kind of wild burdock) preserved in miso
⅜″ (1 cm) thick omelet
2 Tbsp oboro (p.25)
1 tsp toasted white sesame seeds
½ tsp powdered green laver
11½ oz (330 g) sushi rice (p.6)
toasted nori

Preparations: Cut the pokeweed in half. Make a thick omelet as shown on page 43. Cut so that the cross section forms a triangle. Mix oboro to 2⅝ oz (80 g) of sushi rice and make red sushi rice.

---

1   Wings   Body   Eyes

Wings: Cut 1 whole sheet of nori into three pieces across. Leave 1¼″ (3 cm) strip of nori toward your side and ⅜″ (1 cm) on the farthest side and spread 1⅜ oz (40 g) of red sushi rice thereon. Fold into two and shape. Cut ⅜″ (1 cm) off the joint end of nori. Cut in half and pile up. Make two sets of wings.
Body: Roll the thick omelet with ½ sheet of nori.
Eyes: Roll one pokeweed with ½ sheet of nori and add another pokeweed and roll again.

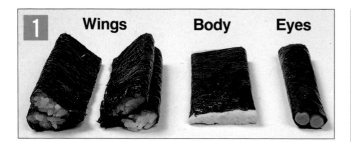

2

Join 1 sheet plus ½ sheet of nori lengthwise with a couple of grains of rice. Leave 1¼″ (3 cm) strip of nori on both sides and spread 4½ oz (130 g) of sushi rice thereon. Place eyes in the center and put ⅓ oz (10 g) of sushi rice on both sides.

3

Place wings on the eyes and let stand the body in the center with the thick end downward.

4

Mix sesame seeds and green laver with 3½ oz (100 g) of sushi rice and cover all. Bring together both ends of nori sheet and roll up. Shape the roll in a cylindrical form.

AGEHACHOO-MAKI
(Butterfly Roll)

Ingredients (1 roll):

8¾″ (22 cm) pokeweed (wild burdock) preserved in miso
shibazuke (assorted vegetables chopped and pickled in salt)
4¼″ (11 cm) takuan (yellow pickled daikon)
shiso-kyurizuke (chopped shiso and cucumber)
⅜″ (1 cm) thick omelet
4¼″ (11 cm) cucumber
5 Tbsp oboro (p.25)
11 oz (310 g) sushi rice (p.6)
toasted nori

Preparations: Cut shibazuke in strips and slice takuan. Cut cucumber in a semicylindrical shape (two). Cook the thick omelet as shown on p.43. Mix oboro with 7¾ oz (220 g) of sushi rice and make red sushi rice.

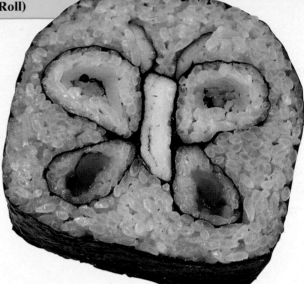

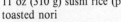

1. Cut a whole sheet of nori into two horizontally: (A) 2⅜″ (6 cm) wide and (B) 3½″ (9 cm) wide.
2. Spread 1 oz (30 g) of sushi rice on nori (A), leaving ⅜″ (1 cm) uncovered at both edges. Lay pokeweed and shibazuke in the center (photo 1). In the same way, spread 2 oz (60 g) of sushi rice on nori (B), and lay takuan and shiso-kyurizuke on top (photo 2).
3. Join the tapering edges together and put 1 oz (30 g) of red sushi rice thereon (photo 3). Cut in half and make wings.

Roll the thick omelet with ½ sheet of nori and make the body.

Join 1 sheet plus ½ sheet of nori lengthwise with sushi rice. Spread 4¼ oz (120 g) of red sushi rice over them, leaving 1¼″ (3 cm) of the nori uncovered on the farther end. Make a mound in the center with ⅓ oz (10 g) of rice and put cucumbers on both sides flanked with ⅓ oz (10 g) rice.

Sandwich the body with wings, and put on [3] as in the photo.

Lift the makisu on one hand, and put 1⅜ oz (40 g) of rice, first, stuffing between the wings (photo 1), then over them to conceal the wings (photo 2). Adjust the roll in a round shape with the makisu.

PANDA-MAKI
(Panda Roll)

Ingredients (1 roll):
½ cod roe (slightly salted)
8¾″ (22 cm) kampyo gourd
4¼″ (11 cm) pickled green leaf stalk
1 small pokeweed (wild burdock) preserved in miso
1 Tbsp furikake (seasoned flour for sprinkling)
3 Tbsp toasted black sesame seeds
15 oz (430 g) sushi rice (p.6)
toasted nori

Preparations: Cook kampyo gourd as shown on p.25. Cut in half. Mix furikake and sesame seeds with 4¼ oz (120 g) of rice and make black sushi rice. Instead of furikake, yukari (powdered shiso leaves) may be used.

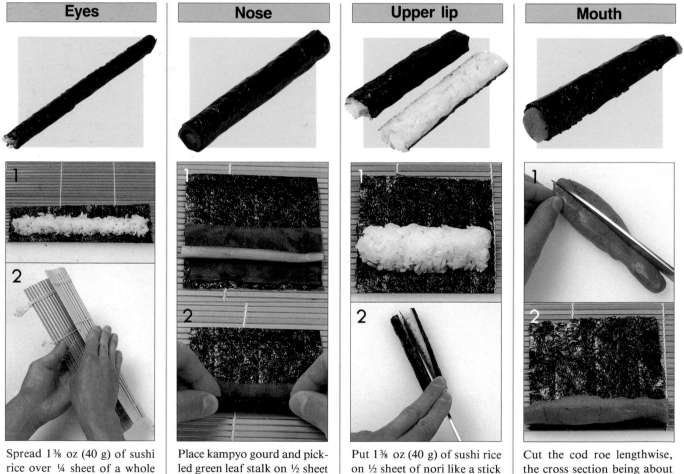

Eyes	Nose	Upper lip	Mouth

Eyes

Spread 1⅜ oz (40 g) of sushi rice over ¼ sheet of a whole sheet of nori horizontally (8¼ × 1¾″) (photo 1), and roll it in a rubbing manner.

Nose

Place kampyo gourd and pickled green leaf stalk on ½ sheet of nori (photo 1), and roll them starting with the edge closer to you.

Upper lip

Put 1⅜ oz (40 g) of sushi rice on ½ sheet of nori like a stick (photo 1), and roll it with the makisu. Cut into two lengthwise with a knife (photo 2).

Mouth

Cut the cod roe lengthwise, the cross section being about ⅜″ (1 cm) (photo 1), place it on the front edge of ½ sheet of nori (photo 2), and roll it up.

1

Spread 2½ oz (70 g) of black sushi rice over ½ sheet of a whole sheet of nori horizontally (8¼ × 3½″) in a thin layer. Put ⅓ oz (10 g) of rice and pile a mound in the center. Place the eye on the mound and roll it in an oval shape. Cut in half.

2

Join 1 sheet plus ½ sheet of nori lengthwise with a few grains of rice. Spread 4¼ oz (120 g) of sushi rice evenly, leaving 1¼″ (3 cm) space at the farthest edge away from you.

3 - 1

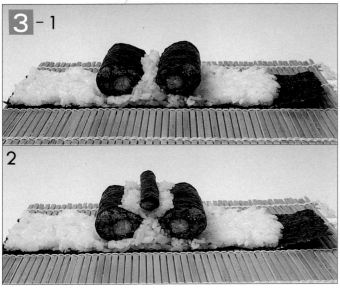

2

Pile a mound in the center with ⅔ oz (20 g) of sushi rice, and place [1] with thinner parts inward (photo 1). Add ⅔ oz (20 g) rice in the center and put the nose on top (photo 2).

4

Add ⅓ oz (10 g) of rice on each eye in the same height of the nose. Put the upper lips on the rice with the cut-part down.

5 - 1

2

Put the mouth between the upper lips and conceal the nori of the upper lips with 1¾ oz (50 g) of rice. Roll all with the makisu and adjust in the round shape (photo 2). Cut into four equal pieces.

6

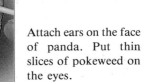

Ears: Spread 1⅜ oz (40 g) of black sushi rice over ½ sheet of nori and roll. Cut in half lengthwise and then into four equal pieces.

7

Attach ears on the face of panda. Put thin slices of pokeweed on the eyes.

TAI-MAKI
(Sea Bream Roll)

Ingredients (1 roll):
4¼″ (11 cm) cooked kampyo (gourd strips)
1 piece thick omelet (¾″ or 2 cm wide)
2 sheets thin omelets
4 Tbsp oboro (p.25)
1 Tbsp yukari (minced salted shiso leaves)
9 oz (260 g) sushi rice (p.6)
toasted nori

Preparations: Cook kampyo gourd as shown on p.25. Cut it into ¼″ (7 mm) width. Prepare two pieces. Cook the thick omelet as on p.43 and the thin omelet as on p.51. Mix oboro with 6 oz (160 g) of rice and make red sushi rice.

Scales	Mouth	Eyes	Tail

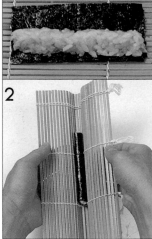

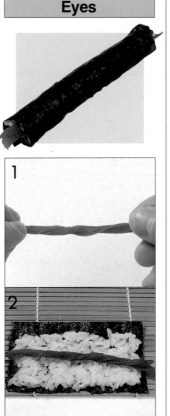

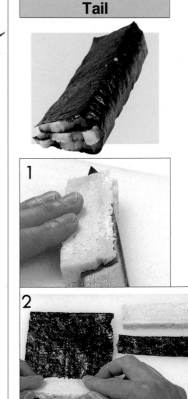

Place ⅓ oz (10 g) of red sushi rice on ¼ sheet of nori (photo 1). Rub the makisu and roll it in a cylinder (photo 2). Make 11 rolls in all.

Place ¼ oz (5 g) of sushi rice on the nori ¾″ (2 cm) wide (photo 1). Double fold. Cut off the seam and make the width ⅜″ (8 mm) (photo 2).

Spread ½ oz (15 g) of sushi rice on ⅓ sheet of nori. Twist the kampyo gourd (photo 1) and place it in the center (photo 2). Roll it in a cylinder.

Cut the thick omelet diagonally, making the thick part ⅜″ (1 cm). The cross section looks a triangle (photo 1). Place ⅔ sheet of nori in between the omelet and roll up (photo 2).

Spread red sushi rice over ⅔ sheet of nori, leaving ¾″ (2 cm) of the far edge uncovered, and pile a mound of rice in the center. Put eyes on the mound and roll in a triangle so that the mound makes a sharp edge.

Make a cut on the mound and put in the mouth. This makes a head.

Combine scales in an isosceles triangle and place in the center of the makisu. Add the head and the tail as shown in the photo below.

Round the makisu on the palm and put 2⅝ oz (80 g) of rice mixed with yukari little by little between the scales and the tail.

Gradually rolling the makisu, put the remaining sushi rice so that the cross section looks round.

Join the thin omelet lengthwise and put [5] on it. Roll the whole starting with the edge closer to you.

Join 1 sheet plus ½ sheet of nori lengthwise using a few grains of rice. (Rice crushed with the thumb forms an adhesive like glue.) Put [6] on it and roll and make the cross section flat.

Put on a cutting board with the design upward. Cut into four equal pieces.

MATSU-MAKI
(Pine Roll)

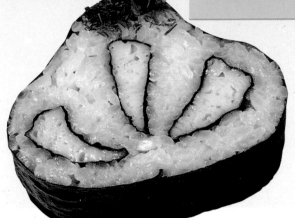

Ingredients (1 roll):
1 thick omelet (¾″ or 2 cm wide)
dash aonori (green laver)
6 oz (160 g) sushi rice (p.6)
toasted nori

Preparations: Cook the thick omelet as shown on p.43.

Cut the thick omelet into four slices so that the cross section looks like a triangle. Use three slices.

Roll each omelet slice with ½ sheet of nori firmly.

Spread 3½ oz (100 g) of sushi rice over 1 sheet of nori, leaving ⅜″ (1 cm) of the nori uncovered on both sides. If desired, yukari (minced salted shiso leaves) or furikake (powdered condiments) may be sprinkled over the rice.

Let one of the omelets stand in the center with the taper upward. Put 1 oz (30 g) of rice on each side.

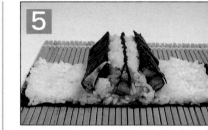

Attach the other omelets on both sides.

Roll it beginning at the side closer to you so that the cross section looks like a flat triangle.

Pinch with fingers and adjust it in a shape of pine. Make the cross section flat.

Cut into four equal parts and decorate with aonori.

TAKE-MAKI

(Bamboo Roll)

Ingredients (1 roll):
3½" (9 cm) cucumber
2⅝ oz (80 g) sushi rice (p.6)
toasted nori

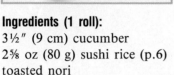

1 Cut the cucumber straight into four thin slices semicylindrically as shown in the photo. (If using a western cucumber adjust size of cucumber slices.)

2 Join two pieces of cucumber with nori inserted in between.

4 Fix the cucumber with fingers and roll, bringing the rice on your side to the rice on the other side.

5 Shape so that the nori between the cucumbers levels with the taper. Cut into 6 equal pieces, and group each three.

3

Place 1 sheet of nori on makisu horizontally and spread 2⅝ oz (80 g) of sushi rice over it, leaving ⅜" (1 cm) of space on both sides. Put the cucumber on the opposite side ⅜" (1 cm) inside from the rice.

SHIPPOO-MAKI

(Cloisonné Roll)

In the same way as the Bamboo Roll, make four rolls in a diamond-shape. With ¾"(2 cm) square of thick omelet core, assemble the four rolls around it and roll the whole with a whole sheet of nori.

UME-MAKI
(Plum Roll)

Ingredients (1 roll):
8¾" (22 cm) kampyo gourd
4¼" (11 cm) cucumber
4¼" (11 cm) pokeweed (wild burdock) preserved in miso
1⅓ Tbsp oboro (p.25)
small amount of red pickled ginger
8⅝ oz (245 g) sushi rice (p.6)
toasted nori

Preparations: Cook kampyo gourd as shown on p.25 and cut in half. Cut cucumber into thin sticks. Mix oboro with 1¾ oz (50 g) of rice and make red sushi rice.

Cut a sheet of nori into four. Lay ⅓ oz (10 g) of red sushi rice on the nori and roll. Make five rolls in all.

Put ½ sheet of nori on the makisu. Lift it with one hand, and assemble [1] around the core of the pokeweed. Roll the whole.

1. Join 1 sheet plus ½ sheet of nori lengthwise and spread sushi rice over it, leaving 1¼" (3 cm) of space on the farthest end. Pile up three mounds with ½ oz (15 g) of rice each from the center toward you (photo 4–1).
2. Place ⅔ sheet of nori in the shape of W and put oboro and red ginger on each indent and top with cucumbers (photo 4–2).
3. Put the branch and flower on either side of the mound (photo 4–3).

Lay kampyo gourd on ⅓ sheet of nori one on top of another. Fold it double. This makes a branch.

Lift the makisu on one hand and put 1 oz (30 g) of sushi rice between the flower and branch. Adjust the roll with the makisu in a semicylinder shape and flatten the cross sections. Cut into four equal pieces.

FUJI-MAKI
(Wisteria Roll)

Ingredients (2 rolls):
3 Tbsp oboro (p.25)
6 oz (160 g) sushi rice (p.6)
toasted nori

Preparations: Mix oboro with sushi rice lightly and make red sushi rice.

HANA-MAKI (Flower Roll)

In the same way as the Wisteria Roll, spread red sushi rice over 1 sheet of nori. Cut cucumber long and thin in a triangle. Put on the farthest end of rice. Roll it up in the shape of a drop of water. Cut it into 6 equal pieces. Assemble all with the cucumber inward.

1 Place 1 sheet of nori on the makisu horizontally. Spread 2⅝ oz (80 g) of red sushi rice over it evenly, leaving ⅜″ (1 cm) space on the farthest end.

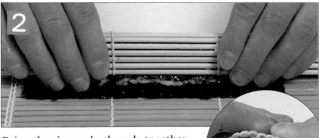

2 Bring the rice on both ends together and roll it in the shape of a drop of water as shown in the photo. Make one more roll.

3 Cut each roll into 8 equal pieces, and group all shifting each other like flowers of wisteria.

TOMOE-MAKI
(Comma-shaped Roll)

Ingredients (1 roll):

1 oz (30 g) tuna (raw red flesh)
3½″ (9 cm) cucumber
3½″ (9 cm) takuan (yellow pickled daikon)

8½ oz (240 g) sushi rice (p.6)
toasted nori

Preparations: Cut tuna into ⅜″ (1 cm) square sticks. Cut cucumber and takuan into thin sticks.

Lay 1 sheet of nori on the makisu horizontally. Spread 2⅝ oz (80 g) of sushi rice evenly, leaving ⅜″ (1 cm) space on the edge closer to you and the other edge. Put one of the ingredients in the center.

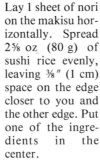

Fold in two so that both edges of nori meet.

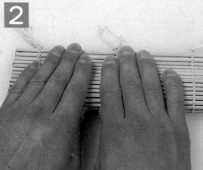

Twist the makisu and adjust it to form a comma-shape. Make other rolls with the other ingredients.

Round the makisu on one hand and put the three rolls, combining the thick part with the thin part. Roll the whole.

Put the roll on a whole sheet of nori, and roll it starting with the edge closer to you. Make the cross sections flat.

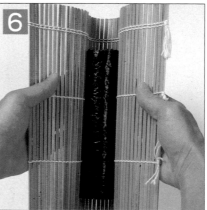

Lift the makisu with both hands, and repeat rolling to form a round shape. Cut into 8 equal pieces.

KIKUSUI-MAKI

(Floating Chrysanthemum Roll)

Ingredients (1 roll):
3 pieces thick omelet (⅜″ or 1 cm wide)
4¼″ (11 cm) pokeweed (wild burdock) preserved in miso
2 Tbsp oboro (p.25)
1 tsp toasted white sesame seeds
7¾ oz (220 g) sushi rice (p.6)
toasted nori

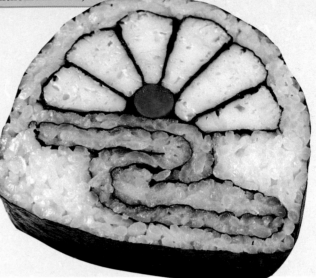

Preparations: Cook thick omelet as shown on p.43. Mix oboro with 2 oz (60 g) of sushi rice and make red sushi rice.

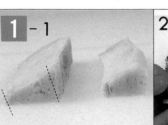

1. Cut the thick omelet in half diagonally. Trim along the dotted lines as shown in the photo above.
2. Roll up each omelet in ½ sheet of nori (photo 1–2).
3. Group six pieces with the pokeweed in the center (photo 1–3). Turn the whole down and set aside.

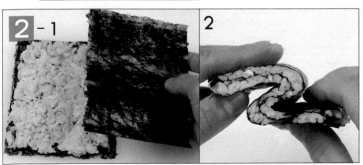

Spread 1 oz (30 g) of red sushi rice over ¾ sheet of nori (4⅛ × 5¼″). Cover with another sheet of nori (photo 2–1). Repeat this again and make them in two tiers. Bend the whole according to the width of the chrysanthemum flower. (photo 2–2).

Put 1 oz (30 g) of sushi rice on both sides of the bend and adjust the shape so that the cross section forms a rectangular.

Join 1 sheet plus ½ sheet of nori lengthwise. Spread 3½ oz (100 g) of sushi rice over them evenly, leaving 1¼″ (3 cm) of space on the side away from you. Sprinkle sesame seeds over the rice and put [3] and [1] together as shown in the photo.

Taking care that it doesn't fall apart, roll up the whole starting with the edge nearest you. Shape it so that it forms an arch with the bottom flat. Make cross sections flat and cut into four equal pieces.

ROKUSHA-MAKI
(Wheel Roll)

Ingredients (1 roll):
1 Tbsp furikake (powdered condiments)
1 Tbsp shiso kyurizuke (minced salted cucumber)
1 Tbsp yukari (minced salted shiso leaves)
1 Tbsp cod roe (lightly salted)
7 oz (200 g) sushi rice (p.6)
1 piece thin omelet
toasted nori

Preparations: Cook thin omelet as shown on p.51. Break cod roe into pieces.

Divide sushi rice into four. Mix with each ingredient lightly.

Lay 2 sheets of nori on the makisu horizontally. Shape two kinds of colored sushi rice into bars and place on each nori.

Roll up starting with the edge closest to you and shape the roll in a round form.

Cut in half. Moisten a sharp knife with water and cut three rolls in half lengthwise. If you cut pressing the knife forward, the roll will not break up.

Lay the thin omelet on the makisu lengthwise. Place the rolls with the cut-side downward. Put the uncut roll in the center.

Supporting with fingers, roll up starting with the edge nearest you. Lift the makisu on both hands and adjust the shape in a round form by rolling.

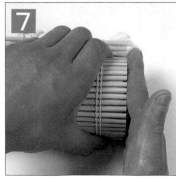

Move the roll to the edge of the makisu and make the cross section flat. Cut into four equal pieces.

SHIKAI-MAKI
(Four Seas Roll)

Ingredients (1 roll):
1¾ oz (50 g) cod roe (lightly salted)
1 piece thick omelet (⅝" or 1.5 cm square)
5¼ oz (150 g) sushi rice (p.6)
toasted nori

Preparations: Cook thick omelet as shown on p.43. Break up the cod roe and mix with sushi rice.

Join 1 and ½ sheets of nori lengthwise with a few grains of rice. Spread red sushi rice over the surface.

Roll up starting with the edge nearest you.

Moisten a sharp knife with water and cut into four lengthwise. If you cut pressing the knife forward, the roll will not break up.

With the thick omelet placed in core, group the rolls with each cut end outward so that it forms a square. Place on 1 sheet of nori lengthwise and roll up starting with the edge nearest you. Adjust the shape and cut into four equal pieces.

HYOOTAN-MAKI
(Gourd Roll)

Ingredients (1 roll):
4¼" (11 cm) pokeweed (wild burdock) preserved in miso
4¼" (11 cm) cucumber
dash shibazuke (assorted vegetables chopped and pickled in salt)
2 stalks mitsuba (honewort)
3½ oz (100 g) sushi rice (p.6)
toasted nori

Preparations:
Cut cucumber and shibazuke into thin sticks. Blanch mitsuba.

Lay 1 sheet of nori on the makisu lengthwise and spread sushi rice over it, leaving ⅜" (1 cm) of space on both edges. Place the pokeweed and cucumber a little above the center, and shibazuke about ⅜" (1 cm) below the edge of rice.

Fold in two at the pokeweed and cucumber.

Join matching the rice of both edges.

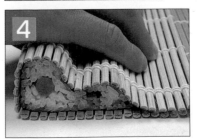

Make a dent between the ingredients and adjust the shape. Cut off extra nori. Cut into four equal pieces and tie each of two pieces with the mitsuba.

THICK & THIN SUSHI ROLLS

Thick sushi rolls are one of the varieties indispensable for picnic lunches and holiday festivities. Thin sushi rolls are arranged with nigiri-zushi assortments or taken as tidbits with alcoholic drinks.

Preparing Ingredients

Kampyo Gourd Strips

Ingredients: ⅞ oz (25 g) kampyo gourd strips / broth (1 cup dashi stock (p.71); 4 Tbsp sugar; 3 Tbsp soy sauce; 1 Tbsp sake; 1 Tbsp mirin added later) / 1 tsp salt

*Dashi stock is prepared with kombu (kelp) and dried bonito.

Method: 1. Wash kampyo gourd strips in water. Rub them with salt until soft (photo 1). Rinse salt off in water, and allow them to stand in freshwater for about 10 minutes.

2. Bring to a boil and cook for 15~20 minutes until a mark made with the finger nail remains (photo 2). Drain in a colander.

3. In a saucepan, pour in the broth (except mirin), add kampyo gourd strips and bring to a boil. Simmer until the liquid is absorbed up to ¼. Add mirin and bring to a boil (photo 3).

4. Let stand in the broth and cool. Cut in about 7″ (18 cm) long.

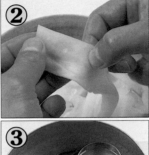

Shiitake Mushroom

Ingredients: 8 dried shiitake mushrooms / broth (1½ cups liquid in which shiitake was soaked; 2 Tbsp sugar; 4 Tbsp each of soy sauce, sake and mirin)

Method: 1. Wash shiitake. Soak in water until soft and discard the stems. Use the water for cooking.

2. Carefully arrange shiitake in a saucepan, and pour in the broth (photo 1). Simmer over low heat about 30 minutes until the liquid has almost evaporated (photo 2).

3. Let stand in the broth and cool. Cut into thin slices.

Oboro

Ingredients: 7 oz (200 g) ground white-flesh fish / 1 Tbsp sugar / 2 Tbsp sake / dash red food coloring

Method: 1. Wrap ground fish in a cloth and wash in water using a squeezing action (photo 1). Change water twice and get rid of fat.

2. Squeeze out excess water and grind in a mortar. Add food coloring dissolved in sake and sugar (photo 2), grind so that the color becomes uniform (photo 3).

3. Transfer to a saucepan and cook over low heat. Mix well with chopsticks until fluffy (photo 4). Spread on a tray and let cool.

Thick Omelet

Cook as shown on page 43 and cut into ⅝″ (1.5 cm) square sticks.

Mitsuba (Honewort)

Blanch a bunch of mitsuba, with special attention to enhancing color, in slightly salted water. Drain in a colander and cool by fanning.

FUTO-MAKI (Thick Sushi Roll)

Divide each ingredient shown on the previous page into three equal parts. Prepare sushi rice as shown on page 6.

①
Lay 1 whole sheet of nori on the makisu lengthwise and spread 10½ oz (300 g) of sushi rice over it, leaving 1¼" (3 cm) of space on the farthest edge. Make a mound on the side away from you so that the ingredients do not stick out.

②
Lightly squeeze juicy ingredients like kampyo gourd strips. Place ingredients in the center with color in mind.

③
Press the ingredients with fingers so that they do not move and lift the side of the makisu closest to you.

④
Bring the sushi rice nearest you to the rice on the far side, rolling up.

⑤
Roll so that the seam comes to the bottom and adjust the shape in a semicylindrical form.

⑥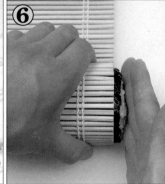
Move the roll to the edge of the makisu and make the cross section flat.

⑦
Moisten a sharp knife and cut into 8 equal pieces.

HOSO-MAKI (Thin Sushi Roll)

Use your favorite ingredients, such as tuna, cucumber, kampyo gourd strips, takuan, etc. Cut kampyo-maki into 4 and the others into 6 equal pieces.

①
Use 1 sheet of nori horizontally. Spread 2⅝ ~ 3½ oz (80 ~ 100 g) of sushi rice over it, leaving ⅜" (1 cm) of space on the farthest edge and ⅛" (5 mm) on the side nearest you.

②
Make a little mound on the farthest side. Place wasabi in the center and the ingredient on it.

③
Lift the end of the makisu and bring the sushi rice nearest you to the sushi rice on the farthest edge.

④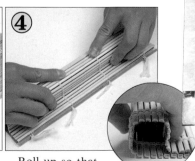
Roll up so that the seam comes to the bottom and shape in a square form.

VARIATIONS OF FUTO-MAKI

Yukiwa-maki (Snow-ring Roll)

Different from ordinary futo-maki, the outside is covered with sushi rice. Cut the ingredients in thin slices or thin sticks to make it easy to roll up.

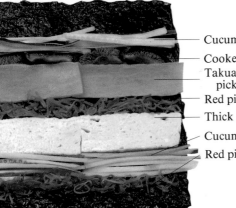

— Cucumber
— Cooked shiitake
— Takuan (yellow pickled daikon)
— Red pickled ginger
— Thick omelet
— Cucumber
— Red pickled ginger

Methods: 1. Cut takuan and thick omelet in thin slices and cucumber into thin sticks.
2. Lay 1 whole sheet of nori lengthwise. Spread 10½ oz (300 g) over it evenly. Sprinkle 2 Tbsp toasted white sesame seeds over the rice (photo 1).
3. Turn it over on a cutting board and place ingredients as shown in the photo. Roll up starting with the edge nearest you (photo 2). Put the seam on the bottom. Wrap it in a plastic wrap and use a makisu to adjust the shape in a semicylindrical form.

Tairyoo-maki (Large Haul Roll)

A jumbo thick sushi roll. Ten kinds of ingredients are rolled up in 1½ whole sheets of nori. Some ingredients are cooked and others are salted, so the roll keeps for a longer time.

— Red salmon roe
— Thick omelet
— Boiled shrimp
— Cucumber
— Crab meat
— Herring roe
— Cooked conger eel
— Cod roe
— Takuan
— Tobiko (Flying fish roe)

Methods: 1. Cut thick omelet in ⅝″ (1.5 cm) wide. Cut cucumber and takuan into thin sticks.
2. Join 1 and ½ whole sheets of nori with a few grains of rice horizontally (photo 1).
3. Spread 14 oz (400 g) of sushi rice over it, leaving ⅜″ (1 cm) of space closest to you and 1¼″ (3 cm) on the farthest edge. Make a mound on the farthest side and spread tobiko and red salmon roe over the rice (photo 2).
4. Place the ingredients as in the photo above, and roll up in the same fashion as shown on the previous page.

NIGIRI-ZUSHI
(Squeezed Sushi)

The exquisite taste of sushi lies in the combination of flavored sushi rice and fresh seafoods. Once you get the knack of the preparation of seafood and how to form sushi rice with toppings, you can enjoy sushi at home.

HOW TO MAKE NIGIRI-ZUSHI

Preparations:

1. Sushi rice
Cook sushi rice as shown on page 6. Let it cool until it reaches body temperature and absorbs vinegar.

2. Ingredients
Arrange them on a tray so that you may use them quickly.

3. Slightly vinegared water
Dampen the fingers with this water so that sushi rice does not stick to your fingers and hands.

Shape about ¾ oz (20 g) of sushi rice into a ball in the right hand. Beginners may make several rice balls in advance.

Place the topping on the flattened fingers of the left hand. Holding the rice ball in your right palm, use the tip of the index finger to place a dab of wasabi in the center of the topping.

Attaching your right index finger to the rice, turn the whole to the right toward the left finger tips.

Replace it in your hand so that the topping faces upward. Press again in the same fashion as in [5].

Holding both sides, turn clockwise and turn 180 degrees.

Inversion method

This method will be applied for sticky toppings like shellfish and squid, and loose toppings like omelets.

Invert your left hand and attaching your right hand turn the whole upside down.

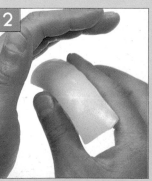

Hold the rice with your right thumb and index finger.

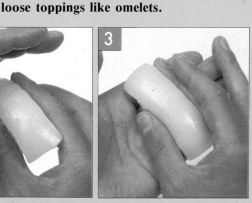

Replace it to the original position. Follow the same procedure.

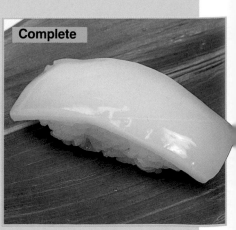

Complete

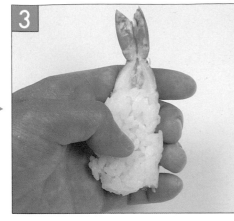

3 Put the rice on the topping. Lightly press the top of the rice with your left thumb so that the center does not become too compact.

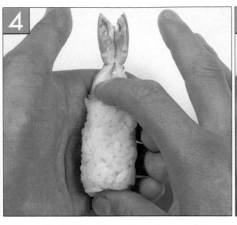

4 Close the left hand gently and press the upper and bottom ends of the rice between the index finger and thumb of your right hand.

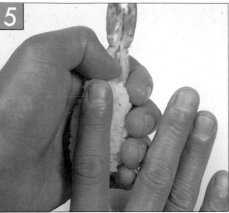

5 Press the three sides of the rice: the upper end with your left thumb, the both sides with your left palm and fingers, and the surface with your right index finger.

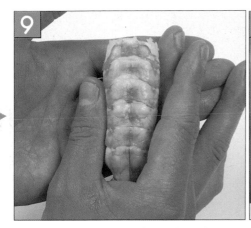

9 Press both sides and shape them flat.

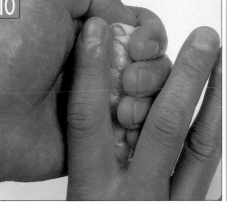

10 Once again press from the three directions, gently squeezing.

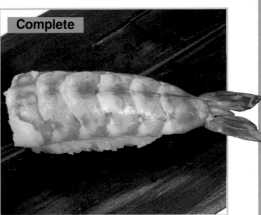

Complete Completed nigiri-zushi. For omelet toppings, wrap in nori, and for conger eel, brush with sauce.

Gunkan-maki
(Battleship Wrap)

Salmon roe or kobashira (adductor muscle in a round clam) is held on top of the rice by a band of toasted nori. When completed, eat while the nori is crispy.

1 Form about ⅞ oz (25 g) of sushi rice into a ball. Cut 1 whole sheet of nori into 6 pieces. Wrap the rice ball in the nori.

2 Fasten the ends together with a grain of rice. Flatten the surface of the rice. Place wasabi on top and cover with the topping.

Complete

TUNA

Tuna for sushi is available in three major varieties: ootoro (heavily marbled with fat), chuutoro (moderately fatty) and akami (red tuna, which is the least oily). Choose your favorite tuna, which is sold in blocks.

Point: Tuna changes color when exposed to the air, so cut it into ½ oz (15 g) slices just before using.

Akami   Chuutoro   Ootoro

▲ Ootoro

▲ Akami

Preparations

▼ Proper cut

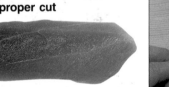

▼ Improper cut

The block of tuna has slanted streaks. Put the knife at right angles to the streaks, and slice so that the streaks become short. Run the knife diagonally downward (photo 1), and then straighten the knife so that it forms a 90° angle with the cutting board and slice off (photo 2). This will make a neat cross section. Squeeze the sushi rice into an oval ball as shown on page 30, and top with the slice.

How to make short slices

Cut the block to 2¾″ (7 cm) long (the width of a hand), and put it on a cutting board lengthwise. Run the knife lengthwise and slice off in the same fashion as on the left.

With tuna

Tekka Sushi in a Bowl   (Tekka-donburi)

Ingredients and method (4 servings):

1. In a saucepan, combine 1 cup each of sake, soy sauce and dashi stock (p.71). Bring to a boil and let cool.

2. Slice 17 oz (480 g) of tuna (akami) as shown above, and marinate the slices in (1) for 30 minutes (photo).

3. Divide 2 lbs (900 g) of the sushi rice (p.6) into four parts and mound each in a serving dish. Drain liquid off the tuna and arrange on top of the rice.

4. Scatter nori over all and top with a shiso leaf, ginger pickled in sweetened vinegar, and wasabi.

SQUID

Among the squids used in sushi are surume-ika (Japanese common squid), yari-ika (spear squid), aori-ika (big fin reef squid), mongoo-ika (common cuttlefish), and sumi-ika (golden cuttlefish). Presented here is a nigiri-zushi, using the body and arms of surume-ika.

Selection: A fresh squid has dark brown skin and shiny black eyes. A stale squid has milk-white skin.

Point: Carefully get rid of moisture and the thin skin inside of the body to keep it fresh.

Arms ▶

▼ Body

■ Removing Arms and Skin

1. With fingers peel the part which joins the body and arms, and take out the arms and the inner organs (photo 1). Remove the cartilage (photo 2). Rinse the inside of the body and wipe dry well.

2. Insert fingers between the body and gills and peel. Pull the gills toward the arms and remove together with the skin (photo 3).

3. Hold with a wet cloth and remove the remaining skin (photo 4).

4. Open the body with a knife (photo 5) and scrape off the slime with the knife. Rub the inside with a dry cloth, and remove the thin skin and moisture (photo 6).

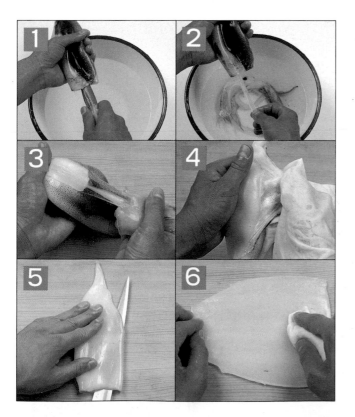

■ Preparations

Body: 1. Trim the four sides and cut into 2¾″ (7 cm) widths. Cut aslant into 1¼″ (3 cm) wide pieces (photo 1).

2. Incise the upper surface with the knife at intervals of ⅜″ (1 cm) (photo 2). Make nigiri-zushi as shown on page 30.

★ Incising makes it easier to eat and season with soy sauce.

Arms: 1. Cut off the entrails just above the eyes. Remove the eyes and the mouth in water and cut off the tips of arms.

2. Boil in hot water until the color changes (photo 1).

3. Cut in half lengthwise and scrape off the suckers (photo 2). Cut aslant into bite-sized pieces. Bind with a strip of nori and coat with *amadare* (p.42).

HORSE MACKEREL

The taste of nigiri-zushi with bluefish toppings is improved if accompanied with ginger, chives and a shiso-leaf.

Selection: Get fresh fish about 6″ (15 cm) long.

Point: Silver-skinned fish such as horse mackerel, shad, and halfbeak should be washed in slightly salted water. If washed in fresh water, they will lose their shine.

Preparations

Cut the fish into three fillets as shown in the photo below. Cut off the center in the shape of V and discard the bone in the center.

Remove the skin from the head toward the tail with one stroke. Wash in lightly salted water and wipe dry.

Make diagonal cross incisions on the surface so that soy sauce can soak in readily.

Construction

When topping with ginger and chives, prepare the rice base without wasabi. Insert them in the incisions.

Cut into Three Fillets

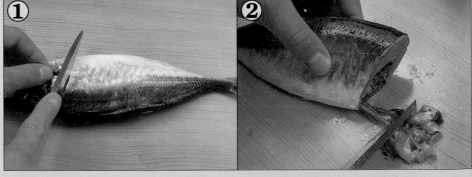

Scale the fish and place on a cutting board with the head pointing toward the left. Insert the knife at the base of the gills and cut off the head.

Insert the point of the knife into the belly and take out the entrails. Wash in lightly salted water and remove the remaining entrails and blood.

MACKEREL

Mackerel easily loses its freshness. In the district where fresh mackerel is available, the raw fish is used for sushi, but generally vinegared mackerel is popular. When raw mackerel is soaked in a seasoned vinegar, the extra water and the smell particular to it are removed.

Selection: Get the mackerel which has clear eyes and the silver skin is bright. Spring and autumn mackerel are best.

Point: The amount of salt and vinegar is a matter of taste. Fatty mackerel should be soaked for a longer time.

How to Make Vinegared Mackerel

Preparations

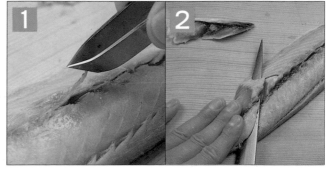

Fillet the mackerel as shown in the photo below. Salt it heavily and allow it to stand for one or two hours.

Rinse in water and wipe dry. Place in a tray, cover with vinegar and allow to stand for 40 minutes or an hour.

By tracing with your finger, pull out the remaining backbone. Remove the thin skin by pulling from the head in the direction of the tail.

Taking care not to break, cut aslant from the tail. Serve with shiso leaves or kombu as you desire.

③ Wipe dry carefully. Insert the knife horizontally just above the backbone and slice all the way along the bone.

④ Turn over the fish so that the backbone comes to the underside. Slice the fish in the same fashion as in (3). As for the use of the bones, see page 75.

⑤ Remove the bones in the belly. Run the knife horizontally and slice aslant.

SEA BREAM & FLOUNDER

◄ Sea Bream

Flounder
▼

ARK SHELL

Taenia ►

Flesh
◄

Sea bream is called the king of fish. It is an ideal fish in shape, taste and color. Get the fish with skin. Pour boiling water over the skin and chill in ice water. This makes the fat between the skin and flesh harden and improves the taste. Flounder is a luxury whitefish. The plain taste and slightly chewy firmness are characteristic of the fish. Citrus fruits and chives will improve the taste of whitefish.

The flesh is bright red because of a high hemoglobin content. The simple taste and firm, resilient flesh are the characteristic of this bivalve mollusk. Since it easily loses freshness, make sure to get a live one.

Preparations

1. Open the shell and cut off the adductor with the knife (photo 1) and take out the flesh.
2. Divide the flesh and taenia (connective filament) (photo 2). Open the flesh with the knife and cut off the black parts (kidney) (photo 3). Discard viscera from the taenia. Rub the flesh and taenia with salt and rinse in water.
3. Make incisions in the thick flesh (photo 4). Fling it at the cutting board to make it firm. Make a nigiri-zushi as shown on page 30. Wrap the taenia nigiri-zushi in nori to make eating easier.

Sea Bream

1. Get fish which is cut into fillets, boned and has skin. Place on a bamboo colander with the skin-side up. Sprinkle a small amount of salt over them (photo 1).
2. Cover with a cloth, pour boiling water over all (photo 2) and then chill in ice water. Wipe dry thoroughly.
3. Place the fillets with the skin-side down, and cut aslant from the tail to ¼″ (7 mm) widths.
4. Make a nigiri-zushi as shown on page 30, and garnish with grated daikon mixed with chili or chives as you desire.

Flounder

Since the flesh is thin, insert the knife almost flat. Place the skin-side down, and cut aslant from the tail. Make a nigiri-zushi as shown on page 30.

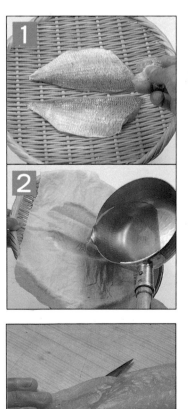

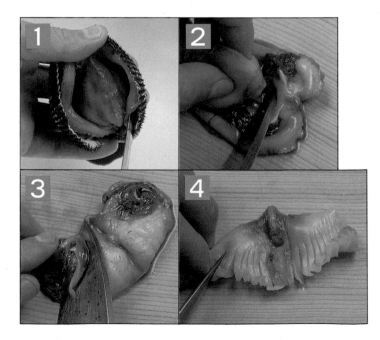

ROUND CLAM

Round clams are called 'aoyagi' in Japanese. The name comes from a village, Aoyagi-mura, in Chiba prefecture, where it abounded. Aoyagi refers to the part which corresponds to the foot and the adductor is called 'kobashira.'

Selection: Get shelled round clams with a taenia to top sushi rice. When only the foot part is available, rinse in salt water and make gunkan-maki (p.31).

Point: Boil round clams in salt water to make firm. Rinse scallops in salt water to remove the sliminess.

◄ Adductor of Round Clam

Round Clam ▶

Round Clam

1. Open the taenia and remove the black viscera (photo 1). Rinse in salt water.
2. Pour mildly salted water in a saucepan with the clams, and place over medium heat. Continue stirring until the water gets hot. This procedure makes the flesh firm (photo 2).
3. Rinse in water. Taking care not to cut off the taenia, make an incision on the underside of the foot (photo 3).
4. Scrape off the viscera with a knife (photo 4) and remove black parts around the taenia (photo 5).
5. Insert the knife in the foot and open it (photo 6). Scrape the underside of the foot and remove the remaining viscera (photo 7).
6. Arrange the taenia in a circular shape (photo 8) and make a nigiri-zushi as shown on page 30.

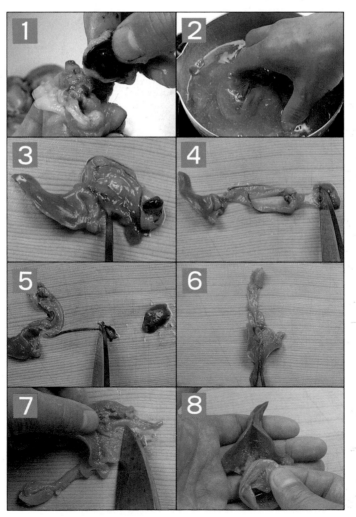

Adductor in a Round Clam

1. Put into a colander. Rinse in mildly salted water (photo 1) and remove sliminess and dirt. Peel off the thin skin on the surface if you desire.
2. Wipe dry and make a gunkan-maki as shown on page 31 (photo 2).

SCALLOP

◀ **Adductor & Taenia**

▼ **Adductor**

The large scallop measures about 8″ (20 cm) in length. In recent years, this bivalve mollusk has been cultivated for the market and is available all year round. The best time, however, is from late autumn to spring. The sweet flavor and the smell of the sea are characteristic of scallops. The chewy firmness of the taenia is also good. Presented here are two kinds of nigiri-zushi: one is topped with the raw scallop and the other with the boiled taenia.

Selection: Get fresh scallops, which close their shells firmly when patted and the taenia seen between shells is moving actively.

Point: Carefully remove the thin skin from the adductor. When boiling, take care not to cook too long.

Adductor

1. Insert the knife between the shells and open (photo 1).
2. Insert the knife under the taenia (photo 2) and take off the adductor gradually.
3. Take the adductor off the taenia and viscera (photo 3).
4. Carefully peel the thin skin off the sides of the adductor (photo 4).
5. Cut the large adductor into 2 or 3 pieces (photo 5). Make an incision in the small one and open (photo 6). Make a nigiri-zushi as shown on page 30.

★ You may bake the taenia as shown on page 77.

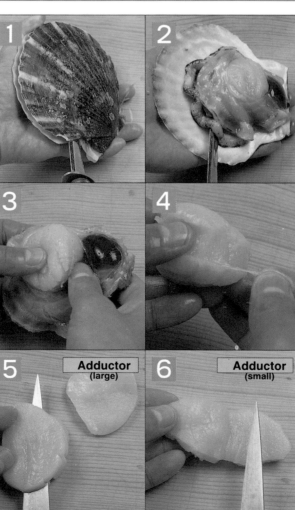

Adductor and Taenia

1. Open the shell as shown in the photo on the left. Cut off the kidney (photo 1) and remove the black string between the taenia.
2. Remove the viscera (photo 2) and cut in half.
3. Pass through slightly salted hot water until it rolls up into a ball (photo 3). Move into ice water. Make a nigiri-zushi as shown on page 30 and coat with amadare (p. 42).

ABALONE & ORMER

The abalone has a spiral shell and is one of the highest-class sushi toppings. The ormer is a small version of abalone, the shell measuring 2″ (5 cm)~3″ (8 cm). Compared with the abalone, the flesh of ormer is harder and less tasty. The abalone is used raw as a nigiri-zushi topping to make the best use of the resilience of the flesh. The ormer is cooked soft.

Selection: Get a fresh one which has thick flesh. The flesh of abalone comes in two colors, black and red. Choose the black one for sushi and sashimi. Use the red one for cooking, steaming and baking.

Ormer ▶

▼Abalone

Abalone

1. Sprinkle salt heavily over the flesh (photo 1). Rub all over with a scrubbing brush (photo 2), removing the sliminess and dirt to make the flesh firm.
2. Rinse in water and wash away salt. Insert a slender metal object between flesh and shell (photo 3).
3. Pull up and out in one stroke and take out the flesh (photo 4).
4. Make a V-shaped incision at the mouth and remove it (photo 5).
5. Cut thinly aslant (photo 6) and make a nigiri-zushi as shown on page 30.

★ If you make shallow incisions on the flesh, it will make eating easier.

Ormer

1. In the same fashion as done for abalone, salt and rub the ormer. Put the whole with the shells in a saucepan. Add water and sake (⅖ of the water) (photo 1), and cook over medium heat for about 20 minutes.
2. Add soy sauce, mirin (sweetened sake) and cook for another 10 minutes.
3. Take out of the shells and remove the viscera. Insert a knife in the flesh and open (photo 2).
4. Make a nigiri-zushi as shown on page 30. Wrap in nori.

SHRIMP

▼ Raw shrimp

Of the many kinds of shrimp, some are used raw and some are boiled for a nigiri-zushi. Prawns and pink shrimp are used raw, and brown shrimp turns a bright pink when cooked.

Selection: Get a fresh prawn about 6″ (15 cm) long. The brown shrimp should be the one bought soon after thawed.

Point: Boil only the tail of the prawn so that it looks attractive. Use bamboo skewers when boiling brown shrimp.

◄ Boiled shrimp ►

Skewer Shrimp to Boil

▲ Before boiling

▲ After boiling

1. Insert a bamboo skewer straight just under the shell into the tail (photo 1).
2. Add a pinch of salt to plenty of boiling water. Add shrimp. When it comes to a boil, cook for about one minute (photo 2).
3. Remove to ice water and chill (photo 3).
4. When chilled completely, draw out the skewer (photo 4). Take care not to draw out while warm, or the shrimp will curl again.

Preparations

Boiled shrimp

1. Trim off the small triangular segment of shell above the tail (photo 1) and shell (photo 2).
2. Neatly cut the head side. Insert the knife deep along the leg side of the shrimp and open (photo 3).
3. Rinse in lightly salted water (use vinegared water in summer) and devein. Make a nigiri-zushi as shown on page 30.

Raw shrimp

1. Put the tail in boiling water and cook until the color changes (photo). Devein with a bamboo skewer.
2. Remove the head and shell. Open. Make a nigiri-zushi as shown on page 30.

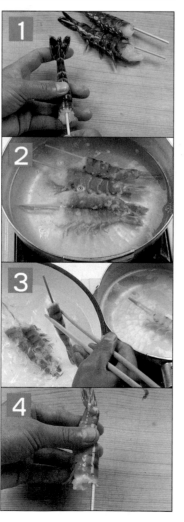

OCTOPUS & SQUILLA

Generally, boiled octopus and squilla are available, but, if possible, get them raw and boil to improve the taste. Boil the octopus from the tips of the arms gradually. In the boiling water add coarse tea so that it brightens the color. The squilla is most tasty when caught in the spawning season, June and July. As time passes, it becomes thinner, so boil as soon as you get it.

Squilla ▶

▼ Octopus

Octopus

1. Insert the knife in the head and cut at the base of arms (photo 1). Turn the head inside out. When turned inside, the movement stops.
2. Cut off the viscera. Sprinkle with salt heavily, squeeze and rub to remove the sliminess (photo 2). Wash away salt and allow it to stand in fresh water for about 10 minutes to remove the salt.
3. Make an incision between the arms (photo 3) so as to be well-shaped when boiled.
4. Add 2 Tbsp, coarse tea wrapped in gauze to sufficient boiling water. Boil the octopus immersing gradually from the tips of arms for about 10~15 minutes (photo 4).
5. Remove to a colander and let cool. Moving the knife up and down, cut aslant. Make a nigiri-zushi as shown on page 30.

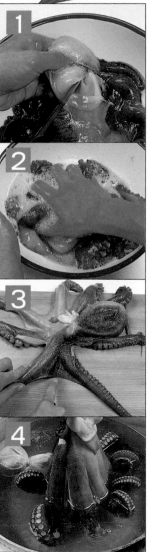

How to cut

Squilla

1. Rinse in water quickly. Boil in plenty of hot water with a pinch of salt added (photo 1).
2. When it comes to a boil, continue cooking for another 2~3 minutes (photo 2), remove to the colander and let cool.
3. Cut off the head, tail and both sides with scissors (photo 3).
4. First, shell the belly-side, holding the flesh with a finger (photo 4), and then the backside.
5. Make a nigiri-zushi as shown on page 30. If you desire, coat it with amadare (p.42).

CONGER EEL

It is difficult to prepare conger eel at home, so buy one prepared at a fish store. Lightly-flavored or grilled conger eel is used for sushi. Cooked conger eel is served coated with amadare, a sweetened dressing made from stock and conger eel bones.

▲ Grilled

▲ Cooked

Ingredients (8 nigiri-zushi):
4 conger eels
Broth:
  2½ cups water
  4⅓ Tbsp sugar
  4⅓ Tbsp sake
  5⅓ Tbsp soy sauce
  1 Tbsp mirin (sweet cooking sake)
salt

Cooked Conger Eel

1. Sprinkle salt lightly over the conger eels and remove the sliminess (photo 1).
2. Rinse in water. Boil in boiling water with a pinch of salt added to remove lye. Insert in the boiling water skin-side first (photo 2) and when it comes to a boil again remove to a bamboo colander (photo 3).
3. In a saucepan add the conger eels, water, sake and sugar (photo 4), and cook over medium heat for about 10~12 minutes. While cooking, add soy sauce (photo 5), and lastly mirin (photo 6) to put on a glaze.
4. Let it stand in the stock until cooled and seasoned well.

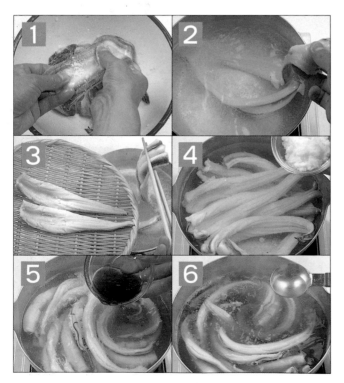

How to Make Amadare (Sweetened Dressing)

1. Grill the bones of the four conger eels slowly until browned over a low-lying medium heat.
2. Add the conger-eel stock (photo 1) and simmer over medium heat until half of the stock evaporates. Strain the stock through cloth (photo 2).
3. Further boil down in a container which is put in boiling water. To test the amadare put a drop of it into a glass of water. If it sinks to the bottom and dissolves, the amadare is perfect.
★Besides the cooked conger eel, the amadare may be used for the squid arms and squillas.

Preparations

Cooked:
Cut diagonally and grill until color changes (photo). Make a nigiri-zushi as shown on page 30. Coat with plenty of amadare and serve.

Grilled:
Remove the sliminess as shown (1) on the left. Grill from the skin-side over a low-lying medium heat (photo). Eat with wasabi.

OMELET

Traditionally, the omelet was made with ground fish meat added, but it is now usually made with dashi stock added.

Point: Mix dashi stock, condiments and eggs and keep in the refrigerator for a half day. This prevents burning.

Ingredients [1 piece of 8¼″ (21 cm) square omelet]:

7 or 8 eggs
⅔ cups dashi stock
2 or 3 Tbsp sugar
1 Tbsp each of sake and mirin (sweet cooking sake)
1 tsp salt
oil for frying

Thick Omelet

1. In a small saucepan, combine dashi stock and condiments and put it over a fire. Stir in sugar and salt with chopsticks and cook until they are dissolved (photo 1).
2. Beat the eggs and add to (1) (photo 2).
3. Oil and heat the square pan. Pour in ¼ of the egg mixture, cook over medium heat and smooth the swelled parts with chopsticks (photo 3).
4. When the surface begins to dry, fold in two steps toward you (photo 4).
5. Oil the pan again and pour in the remaining mixture in three times. Allow the mixture to flow beneath the cooked eggs (photo 5) and roll up.
6. Adjust the shape at the corner of the pan (photo 6).

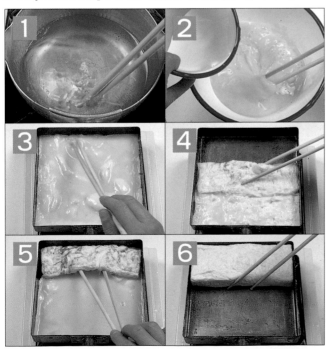

How to Make a Nigiri-zushi

Method 1

Cut the thick omelet in ¾″ (2 cm) widths. Make a deep incision lengthwise. Stuff ⅓ oz (10 g) of sushi rice (p.6) and tie with cooked kampyo (p.25) or boiled mitsuba (honewort).

Method 2

Cut the thick omelet in ¾″ (2 cm) widths. Make an incision in the center. Stuff with a small amount of oboro (p.25) and ¼ oz (7 g) of sushi rice (p.6). Cut into half and wrap in nori.

Method 3

Cut the thick omelet in ⅜″ (1 cm) widths and make a nigiri-zushi as shown on page 30. Tie with a strip of nori. The sushi rice base should be smaller than for that used with fish and shell toppings.

GUNKAN-MAKI (Battleship Wrap) with toppings which suit your taste

Matsumae-zuke

Ingredients (1 roll) & method: Squeeze ⅞ oz (25 g) of sushi rice (p.6) into a small patty and wrap in toasted nori. Dab with wasabi and top with a proper amount of matsumae-zuke.
★Matsumae-zuke is squid and kombu preserved in sake and soy sauce. For variations, use sea urchin and herring roe.

Kani-ko

Ingredients (1 roll) & method: Squeeze ⅞ oz (25 g) of sushi rice (p.6) into a small patty and wrap in toasted nori. Dab with wasabi and top with a proper amount of kani-ko.
★Kani-ko is salted crab eggs. Eggs of shrimp, flying fish, and smelt are also used in the same fashion.

Cod Roe

Ingredients (1 roll) & method: 1. Remove the thin skin from the lightly-salted cod roe and mix with a small amount of sake.
2. Squeeze ⅞ oz (25 g) of sushi rice (p.6) into a small patty and wrap in toasted nori. Dab with wasabi and top with cod roe to fill.

Sea Urchin Roe

Choose small grains of roe which are uniform, and well-shaped. Most of the imported roe is large, has a strong smell and tastes bitter because of preservatives or alum.
Ingredients (1 roll) & method: Squeeze ⅞ oz (25 g) of sushi rice (p.6) into a small patty and wrap in toasted nori. Dab with wasabi and top with raw sea urchin roe to fill.

Salmon Roe

Choose moderately salted large roe.
Ingredients (1 roll) & method: Squeeze ⅞ oz (25 g) of sushi rice (p.6) into a small patty and wrap in toasted nori. Dab with wasabi and top with salmon roe to fill.

✳**See page 31 for forming a nigiri-zushi.**

①Matsumae-zuke ②Kani-ko ③Cod roe
④Sea urchin roe ⑤Salmon roe

VARIATIONS OF NIGIRI-ZUSHI with toppings other than seafood

Avocado

Ingredients (1 roll) & method: 1. Cut an avocado in half lengthwise, remove seeds and pare. Cut the flesh into eight bite-size slices.
2. Squeeze ⅔ oz (20 g) of sushi rice (p.6) into a small patty and top with a slice of avocado. Bind the whole thing with a thin strip of toasted nori.

Ham & Tomato

Ingredients (1 roll) & method: 1. Squeeze ⅔ oz (20 g) of sushi rice (p.6) into a small patty and wrap in ½ piece of ham. Bind the whole thing with a thin strip of toasted nori.
2. Garnish with a slice of cherry tomato and mayonnaise.

Grilled Shiitake Mushroom

Ingredients (1 roll) & method: 1. Discard the stem of a shiitake mushroom.

Season with 1 Tbsp each of soy sauce and mirin (sweet cooking sake) and grill.
2. Squeeze ⅔ oz (20 g) of sushi rice (p.6) into a small patty and top with the shiitake. Bind the whole thing with a thin strip of toasted nori.

Mountain Yam
(Yama Imo)

Ingredients (1 roll) & method: 1. Pare the yam and plunge in vinegared water to prevent color change. Grate it.
2. Squeeze ⅞ oz (25 g) of sushi rice (p.6) into a small patty and wrap in a band of toasted nori. Dab with wasabi and place ½ piece of green shiso leaf on top. Top with a proper amount of grated yam and a quail's egg.

Pickled Green Leaf

Ingredients (1 roll) & method: 1. Squeeze ⅞ oz (25 g) of sushi rice (p.6) into a small patty and wrap in a piece of pickled green leaf.
2. Bind with a thin strip of takuan (yellow pickled daikon).

①Avocado ②Ham & Tomato
③Grilled Shiitake
④Mountain Yam
⑤Pickled Green Leaf

*See pages 30 and 31 for forming a nigiri-zushi.

Nigiri-zushi for children
MINI-NIGIRI & ANIMAL-NIGIRI

Mini-Nigiri (1 serving)
Ingredients & method: 1. Form 2 oz (60 g) of sushi rice (p.6) into a bar (photo 1). Cover with plastic wrap and adjust the shape with a makisu (bamboo mat). Cut bar and wrap together into bite-size pieces (photo 2).
2. Cut any ingredients you like into the same size as the sushi patty and bind with a strip of toasted nori (photo 3).

Rabbits Squid (2 rolls)
Ingredients & method: 1. Cut the four corners off the two pieces of squid body [1¼″ (3 cm) × 2⅜″ (6 cm) each] (photo 1).
2. Cut the longer edges of a piece of squid body [1½″ (4 cm) × 1¼″ (3 cm)] diagonally (photo 2). Fold in half with a thin slice of tuna in the center. Cut into four equal pieces and make the ears (photo 3).
3. Divide 1⅜ oz (40 g) of sushi rice (p.6) into two. Squeeze each into a small patty and top with (1). Put ears on it, eyes of salmon roe and mouth of a slice of cucumber.

Carp Shrimp (2 rolls)
Ingredients & method: 1. Boil and open two pieces of shrimp as shown on page 40. Squeeze 1⅜ oz (40 g) of sushi rice (p.6) into two patties.
2. Top with the shrimp. Make eyes with the suckers of boiled octopus and pectoral and tail fins with slices of cucumber.

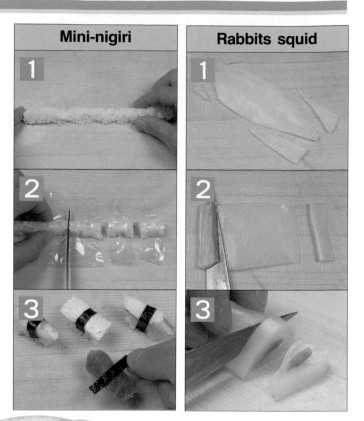

Mini-nigiri
Rabbits squid

1
1
2
2
3
3

How to Arrange Nigiri-zushi

Three kinds of arrangements in traditional serving containers are shown. Plates and trays may be used instead at home.

One serving

Arrange nigiri-zushi closer to you and hoso-maki (thin rolls) horizontally further away from you. Separate those with raw toppings and cooked ones. Add one gunkan-maki. Set the thin rolls so that the seam of nori faces the back. Garnish with ginger preserved in sweetened vinegar and decorate with a bamboo leaf. For one serving, arrange 6~8 nigiri-zushi, and 1 roll of hoso-maki.

Many servings

Arrange each individual serving in a radial pattern so that it can be taken from any direction. Place hana-maki (p.19) instead of hoso-maki to give a flowery atmosphere, and arrange nigiri-zushi and hoso-maki with color in mind.

A three-dimensional arrangement with shrimp rested against omelets in the center. The sushi is assorted symmetrically according to the ingredients. It is unsightly to fill up the container with sushi, so it is not necessary to arrange one piece of each per person.

A VARIETY OF ATTRACTIVE SUSHI

Sushi is enjoyed with the eye as well as the palate. Introduced are popular chirashi-zushi, delicious inari-zushi, novel bou-zushi and oshi-zushi, and fancy sushi loved by children.

CHIRASHI-ZUSHI
(Scattered Sushi)

Chirashi-zushi is a bowl of sushi rice on which a variety of flavored, cooked, or raw ingredients are scattered colorfully. Introduced here are three kinds of orthodox chirashi-zushi with seafood and a Western-style chirashi-zushi for young people.

CHIRASHI WITH CONGER EEL

Ingredients (4 servings):

4 conger eels
Stock:
  2½ cups water
  4⅓ Tbsp sugar
  4⅓ Tbsp sake
  5⅓ Tbsp soy sauce
  1 Tbsp mirin (sweet
  cooking sake)
oil for frying

Thin omelet:
  1 egg
  1 egg yolk
  1 Tbsp sake
  1 tsp salt
  1 Tbsp cornstarch
2 lbs (900 g) sushi rice (p.6)
a bunch of mitsuba (honewort)
salt

Method: 1. Get prepared conger eel at a fish store. Sprinkle with salt and remove the sliminess as shown on page 42. Cook in stock until soft. Make amadare by adding grilled bones to the broth and boiling down (p.42). Let the flesh cool completely and cut into roughly ⅜″ (1 cm) widths.
2. Blanch mitsuba in lightly salted water. Transfer to a bamboo colander and fan to cool. Squeeze out liquid and cut into ¾″ (2 cm) lengths.
3. Cook the thin omelet as shown below. Roll it up and cut into thin strips (kinshi-tamago).
4. Mound sushi rice in a container. Top with egg strips, and scatter conger eels and mitsuba all over. Coat conger eels with amadare.
★ Add cornstarch to the beaten egg to make a perfect thin omelet spread.

EDOMAE-CHIRASHI (Seafoods)

Ingredients (4 servings):

4 slices akami (red tuna flesh)
4 slices chuutoro (medium fatty tuna)
4 slices amberjack
2 horse mackerels
4 slices squid
4 round clams
4 shrimps
2 cooked conger eels (p.42)
1½″ (4 cm) thick omelet (p.43)
3 or 4 cooked kampyo gourd strips (p.25)
4 Tbsp oboro (p.25)
4 cooked shiitake mushrooms (p.25)

a small amount of lotus root
Sweetened vinegar:
  ¼ cup vinegar
  1 Tbsp sugar
  2 Tbsp water
4 slices kamaboko (boiled fish paste)
2 lbs (900 g) sushi rice (p.6)
shredded nori
green shiso leaves
slices of cucumber
wasabi
sweet-sour pickled ginger

Method: 1. Cut the amberjack aslant. Prepare other seafoods and thick omelet as shown on pages 32~43.
2. Chop the cooked kampyo gourd strips. Make a cross incision on the top of the cooked shiitake mushrooms. Pare the lotus root and cut into thin slices. Blanch and allow them to stand in the sweetened vinegar to season.
3. Arrange the ingredients as shown below, and garnish with decorative slices of cucumber (p.79), wasabi and pickled ginger stalks.

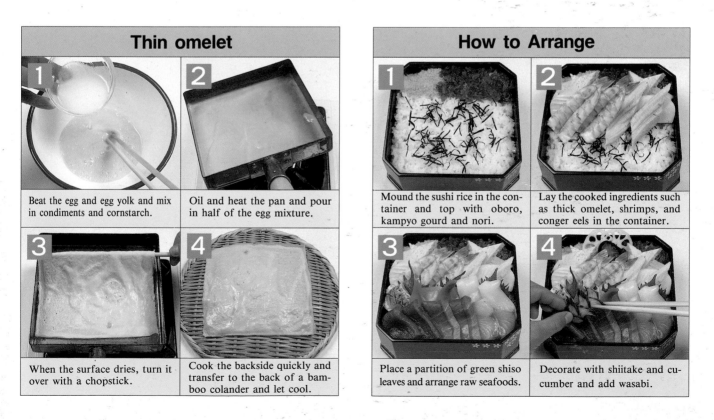

Thin omelet

1. Beat the egg and egg yolk and mix in condiments and cornstarch.

2. Oil and heat the pan and pour in half of the egg mixture.

3. When the surface dries, turn it over with a chopstick.

4. Cook the backside quickly and transfer to the back of a bamboo colander and let cool.

How to Arrange

1. Mound the sushi rice in the container and top with oboro, kampyo gourd and nori.

2. Lay the cooked ingredients such as thick omelet, shrimps, and conger eels in the container.

3. Place a partition of green shiso leaves and arrange raw seafoods.

4. Decorate with shiitake and cucumber and add wasabi.

CHOPPED BONITO-ZUSHI

Ingredients (4 servings):

14 oz (400 g) bonito
Marinade:
  ¼ cup sake
  ¼ cup soy sauce
  ginger juice (squeezed from
  ½ piece)

1 naga-negi (leek) (white part)
1 ginger root
a bunch of chives
some benitade
  (red smartweed)
2 lbs (900 g) sushi rice (p.6)

It is said that fishermen on board a skipjack fishing vessel created this sushi. A large amount of strong smelling naga-negi and ginger are used to modify the particular smell of the bonito.

Method: 1. Combine sake and soy sauce in a small saucepan and bring to a boil. Chill completely and then add ginger juice.
2. Get bonito prepared for sushi at a fish store. Cut off any bloody colored flesh (photo 1) and cut into bite-size pieces. Soak in marinade for 20 to 30 minutes to season (photo 2).
3. Drain the bonito and scatter it over sushi rice prepared as shown on page 6, mixing well with fingers (photo 3). The point is to mix quickly and thoroughly before the rice becomes sticky.
4. Cut the naga-negi into 2″ (5 cm) lengths. Make an incision lengthwise and remove the hard part in the center. Cut into thin strips (photo 4) and rinse in water. Grate ginger and chop chives.

5. Mound sushi rice mixed with bonito on a container and scatter naga-negi, ginger, chives and red smartweed over all colorfully.

Western-style Marinated Beef Sushi

Ingredients (4 servings):

11 oz (300 g) ~ 14 oz
  (400 g) round of beef
Marinade:
  1 cup water
  1 bouillon cube
  ¼ cup sake
  ¼ cup soy sauce
2 lbs (900 g) sushi rice (p.6)
5 lettuce leaves

1 cucumber
½ lemon
½ onion
some cherry tomatoes
some chrysanthemum
  flowers
1 Tbsp oil for frying
salt and pepper

Method: 1. Combine all the ingredients of marinade in a small saucepan and bring to a boil. Dissolve the bouillon cube and let cool.

2. Rub salt and pepper into the round of beef (photo 1) and set aside for about 20 minutes to season.

3. Heat and oil a skillet and roll the round of beef until the surface is browned (photo 2).

4. Transfer into ice water and allow it to stand about 10 minutes (photo 3). This procedure chills the meat and removes the extra fat.

5. Wipe dry and soak in the marinade for 30 to 40 minutes (photo 4).

6. Tear the lettuce leaves into bite-size pieces, cut the cucumber into thin slices diagonally, the lemon into thin semicirculars slices, and the tomato decoratively. Cut the onion into thin round slices, season with salt and rinse in water.

7. Mound the sushi rice on a plate, top with thin slices of beef and garnish with vegetables and chrysanthemum flowers.

INARI-ZUSHI
(Sushi Rice in Fried Tofu Bags)

The salty-sweet abura-age (fried tofu bag) and savory sour sushi rice give a harmony of delicious taste. Introduced here are a basic inari-zushi and two kinds of variations.

INARI-ZUSHI

Ingredients (8 pieces):

4 abura-age (fried tofu bags)
Stock:
  1½ cups water
  4 Tbsp sugar
  5 Tbsp soy sauce
  2 Tbsp sake
  4 Tbsp mirin (sweet cooking sake)

11½ oz (320 g) sushi rice
3 Tbsp toasted white sesame seeds
sweet-sour pickled ginger stalks

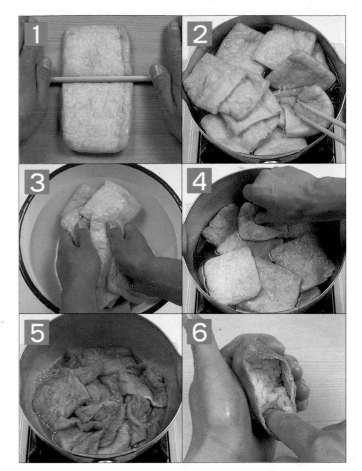

Method: 1. Place abura-age lengthwise on a chopping board. Roll with a chopstick to make it easy to open (photo 1). Cut in half crosswise and make 8 pieces. Open at one end with care not to tear them.
2. Blanch in plenty of boiling water and remove the fat (photo 2). Rub in water as if washing clothes (photo 3) and squeeze water completely out.
3. In a saucepan, combine the stock ingredients and bring to a boil. Add abura-age (photo 4), place a small lid directly on it, and simmer over low heat about 15 to 20 minutes until almost all the liquid has evaporated (photo 5). Remove from the heat and let cool in the stock. Transfer to a bamboo colander.
4. Cook sushi rice as shown on page 6 and mix in toasted sesame seeds.
5. Fill each tofu bag with equal amount of sushi rice. Fill firmly to the edges (photo 6) and tuck opening flaps inward.

★Sushi rice may be mixed with green shiso leaves cut in julienne, dried young sardines, hemp seeds, cooked kampyo gourd strips, shiitake mushrooms and so on.

YOTTO-INARI
(Sailboat-inari)

Ingredients (8 pieces):

8 cooked abura-age (fried tofu bags)
8 tsp oboro (p.25)
3″ (8 cm) takuan (yellow pickled daikon)

some benishoga (red pickled ginger)
some cucumber
11½ oz (320 g) sushi rice

Method: 1. Cook abura-age as above, oboro as shown on page 25 and sushi rice as shown on page 6.
2. Cut takuan into round slices ⅛″ (5 mm) wide. Make the sail and rudder of the sailboat with the skin of cucumber.
3. Tuck the opening flaps of the abura-age about ⅜″ (1 cm) inward. Mold sushi rice into 8 balls and fill them into each abura-age (photo).
4. Top with oboro, takuan, ginger and decorate with cucumber.

SHINODA-MAKI
(Shinoda Rolls)

Ingredients (16 rolls):

8 cooked abura-age (fried tofu bags)
24″ (60 cm) pickled green leaf stalk

16 mitsuba (honewort)
14 oz (400 g) sushi rice (p.6)
3 Tbsp toasted white sesame seeds

Method: 1. Cook abura-age as shown above. Cut edges off and open to make a flat sheet.
2. Cut the green leaf stalk to match with the width of the abura-age. Blanch mitsuba.
3. Cook sushi rice as shown on page 6. Mix in toasted sesame seeds.
4. Place sushi rice on the abura-age (photo), and roll it up with the green leaf stalk in the center.
5. Tie two places with mitsuba and cut in half.

BOU-ZUSHI
(Bar-shaped Sushi)

Form sushi rice in the shape of a bar, top with ingredients, and adjust the shape with plastic wrap and a makisu. Different from maki-zushi, it is easier and simpler to make. Combine any ingredients as you like, and enjoy your own taste.

TAZUNA-ZUSHI
(Rein Sushi)

Ingredients (1 roll):

2½″ (7 cm) takuan (yellow
  pickled daikon)
2 kani-fuumi-kamaboko
  (crab-flavored fish paste)
1 green shiso leaf
3½ oz (100 g) sushi rice (p.6)

some shibazuke (assorted
  vegetables chopped and
  pickled in salt)
1 Tbsp toasted white sesame
  seeds

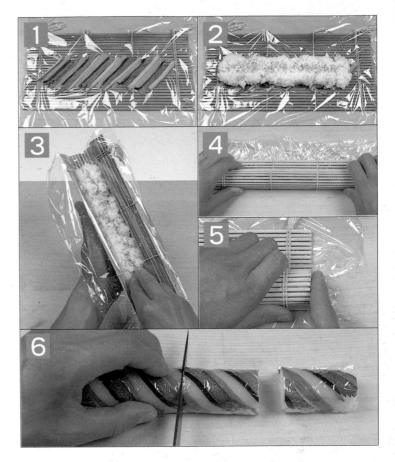

Method: 1. Cut takuan into thin slices. Cut takuan, the green shiso leaf and shibazuke together into 2½″ (7 cm) long thin strips. Peel the red strip off the surface of kamaboko.
2. Cook sushi rice as shown on page 6.
3. Lay plastic wrap on a makisu for thin rolls. Arrange the ingredients (1) diagonally with color in mind (photo 1).
4. Top with sushi rice in the shape of a bar, and sprinkle sesame seeds over it (photo 2).
5. Hold the makisu in both hands and make it round (photo 3). Wrap it in plastic wrap and form it into a semicylindrical shape with the makisu (photo 4).
6. Move it to the edge of the makisu and make the cross section flat (photo 5).
7. Cut it together with the wrap into bite-size pieces (photo 6). Remove the wrap and serve.
★Colorful sushi perfect for serving guests. Other ingredients recommended for combination are halfbeak, boiled shrimp, thin omelet, and cucumber.

HORSE MACKEREL BOU-ZUSHI

Ingredients (1 roll):

1½ horse mackerel
2 green shiso leaves
1 clove ginger

3½ oz (100 g) sushi rice (p.6)
salt
vinegar

Method: 1. Cut the horse mackerel into fillets and remove the backbone in the shape of V (p.34). Soak in saltwater for about 20 minutes. Rinse in freshwater and wipe dry. Cover with vinegar diluted by 10% water. Allow it to stand for about 15 minutes. Remove skin from head to tail.
2. Form sushi rice in the shape of a bar. Top with the head and tail of the horse mackerel alternately. Cover with plastic wrap and adjust the shape with the makisu (photo).
3. Cut it together with the wrap and garnish with green shiso leaves cut into julienne strips and grated ginger.

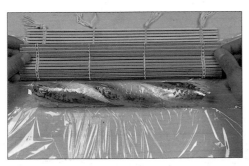

SHRIMP & CRAB BOU-ZUSHI

Ingredients (1 roll):

2½ shrimps
5 pieces crab meat
dash cucumber
dash lemon peel

3½ oz (100 g) sushi rice (p.6)
½ tsp lemon juice
salt

Method: 1. Boil shrimps as shown on page 40. Open and cut off the tail and cut in half lengthwise. Cut the skin of cucumber in thin strips and soak in saltwater until soft. Cut lemon quarters into slices.
2. Mix lemon juice with sushi rice. Form the rice in the shape of a bar.
3. Top with shrimps, crab meat, cucumber, and lemon colorfully as shown in the photo. Cover with plastic wrap, adjust the shape with the makisu and cut into bite-size pieces.

OSHI-ZUSHI
(Pressed Sushi)

This Kansai-style sushi is made in a wooden mold pressed with weights. By applying pressure the sushi rice and ingredients harmonize and give a mild taste. When the special mold is not available, make use of a rectangular pan or a lunch box.

SMALL SEA BREAM OSHI-ZUSHI

Ingredients [for 8¹/₄″(21 cm) × 3″(8 cm) × 2″(5 cm) mold]:

12 vinegared small sea bream
(available on the market)
14 oz (400 g) sushi rice (p.6)
1 tsp yukari (minced salted shiso
leaves)
sudori-shoga (sweet-sour pickled
ginger stalk)

★The vinegared small sea bream is
sold at stores under the name of
'kodai no sasazuke.' It consists of
fillets of sea bream preserved in vinegar together with bamboo leaves,
which have a preservative effect.

Method: 1. Soak the wooden mold in water so that sushi rice does not stick to it (left photo).
2. Wipe the mold dry and pack the sea bream tightly all over the bottom of the frame (photo 1).
3. Mix sushi rice with yukari. Spread a layer of sushi rice on top of the sea bream. Take care to fill the rice compactly so that there will be no space in the four corners. Cover with an aspidistra leaf or plastic wrap (photo 2).
4. Place the lid on top and press the whole through the mold (photo 3).
5. Turn over, remove the bottom, and cut into bite-size pieces (photo 4). Arrange on a serving platter and garnish with ginger stalks.

EEL OSHI-ZUSHI

Ingredients [for 8¹/₄″(21 cm) × 3″(8 cm) × 2″(5 cm) mold]:

½ broiled eel
1 pack sauce for eel (sold
together with eel)
14 oz (400 g) sushi rice (p.6)

Thin omelet:
1 egg
1 egg yolk
1 Tbsp sake
1 tsp salt
1 Tbsp cornstarch

Method: 1. Pour sauce over the eel and heat it in a microwave oven. Cut in half lengthwise.
2. Cook thin omelets as shown on page 51. Cut one of them into thin strips.
3. Spread the eel and omelet in the bottom of the mold. Top with the sushi rice. Press as shown on the left. Cut into bite-size pieces.

TRI-COLOR OBORO-ZUSHI

Ingredients [for 6″(15 cm) × 4³/₄″(12 cm) × 1¹/₂″(4 cm) mold]:

Meat oboro:
3½ oz (100 g) ground beef
2 Tbsp sugar
1 Tbsp sake
1 Tbsp soy sauce
some oil for frying
5 Tbsp oboro (p.25)

Egg oboro:
1 egg
1 egg yolk
1 Tbsp sugar
1 tsp sake
dash salt
10½ oz (300 g) sushi rice (p.6)
2 Tbsp toasted black sesame
seeds

Method: 1. Meat oboro: combine ground meat and other ingre-dients and stir-fry in an oiled skillet. Continue stirring over medi-um heat. Stop the heat just before the liquid has evaporated. Transfer to a plate.
2. Egg oboro: combine eggs and other ingredients. In a small saucepan make scrambled eggs and strain them.
3. Make oboro as shown on page 25. Cook sushi rice as shown on page 6 and mix with sesame seeds.
4. Place aluminum foil on the inside of the mold and spread a layer of sushi rice compactly without leaving any space in the four corners.
5. Put three kinds of oboro diagonally in ³/₈″ (1 cm) widths. Use a sheet of paper to neatly arrange ingredients (right photo).
6. Place aluminum foil on it and press with the bottom of the mold of the same size. Cut into bite-size pieces.

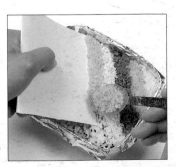

FANCY SUSHI

Form various shapes with sushi rice and make fantastic sushi. Introduced here are flowery sushi prepared with seafoods, sushi for the Doll's Festival, Christmas, and many other attractive sushi.

Pomegranate Sushi

Camellia Sushi

Sushi Dumplings

Red & White Plum Sushi

POMEGRANATE SUSHI

Ingredients (1 piece each):

1 tsp oboro (p.25)
1 green shiso leaf
⅓ oz (10 g) red salmon roe

2 oz (60 g) sushi rice (p.6)
2 sheets toasted nori 3¼″ (8 cm) square

Wrap sushi rice in nori and form it into a ball. Make incisions so that it looks like a ripe pomegranate with the thick skin cracked.

Method: 1. Cut off a bit of the four corners of nori. Divide sushi rice in two equal parts and form each into a ball.

2. Oboro sushi: Place the nori on plastic wrap. Add the shiso leaf and oboro in this order. Put the sushi rice ball in the center (photo). Bring the four corners of the wrap together and form it into a ball. Make incisions crosswise and open lightly.

3. Salmon roe sushi: Put the sushi rice on the nori. Bring the four corners of the wrap together and form it into a round shape. Make incisions crosswise and fill them with the salmon roe.

RED & WHITE PLUM SUSHI

Ingredients (1 piece each):

5 slices tuna [1¼″ (3 cm) square]
5 slices squid [1¼″ (3 cm) square]

small amount of kimi-soboro (★)
3½ oz (100 g) sushi rice (p.6)
toasted nori

Make the red blossom of plum with tuna and the white blossom with squid.

Method: 1. Diagonally cut off the four corners of tuna and squid (photo 1). Divide sushi rice into 10 parts and form each into a ball. Put tuna and squid slices on each rice ball.

2. Cover each of the 5 balls separately with plastic wrap and form each into a round shape (photo 2).

3. Assemble the 5 balls together, encircle with a ½″ (1.5 cm) wide band of nori, and top with kimi-soboro.

★Kimi-soboro is the finely grated yolk of an hard-boiled egg.

CAMELLIA SUSHI

Ingredients (1 piece):

6 pieces smoked salmon
small amount of takuan (yellow pickled daikon)
1 green shiso leaf

1¾ oz (50 g) sushi rice (p.6)
small amount of toasted nori

Method: 1. Roll up the smoked salmon piece by piece and make the petals of the camellia (photo 1).

2. Form the sushi rice into a round shape with a flat top. Encircle it with a band of nori.

3. Place the shiso leaf and top with the salmon (photo 2). Complete by inserting julienne strips of takuan in the center.

SUSHI DUMPLINGS

Ingredients (2 sets):

2 slices tuna [1¼″ (3 cm) square]
2 slices squid [1¼″ (3 cm) square]

1 shrimp
3½ oz (100 g) sushi rice (p.6)
small amount of green shiso leaf

Method: 1. Boil the shrimp as explained on page 40. Open and remove the tail. Cut into 1¼″ (3 cm) square. Diagonally cut off the four corners of tuna, squid and shrimp as done above.

2. Divide sushi rice into 6 parts and form each into a ball.

3. Place the seafood on a piece of plastic wrap and put the rice ball on it (photo). Bring the wrap together and squeeze into a round shape.

4. Place thin strips of shiso leaf on the squid. Skewer all three kinds of dumplings for each serving.

HINA DOLL SUSHI

Emperor

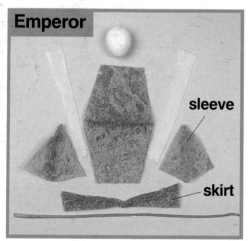

sleeve

skirt

Ingredients & method:
1. Prepare 2 abura-age cooked as explained on page 55. Cut both edges of one of them diagonally and open. The cut-off one makes a skirt. Cut the other into a small triangle and open. This makes sleeves.
2. Boil a quail egg and a stalk of mitsuba (honewort). Mix 2½ oz (70 g) of sushi rice (p.6) with 1 Tbsp furikake (powdered condiments).
3. Form 2 oz (60 g) of sushi rice into a semicylindrical shape and cover with abura-age. Put two strips of thin omelet on it and tie with mitsuba (honewort). Place the skirt of abura-age in front. Fill each sleeve of abura-age with ¼ oz (5 g) of sushi rice (photo). Place them on both sides.

4. Insert a toothpick in the quail egg and fasten it through the body. Make the face and hair with toasted nori and the crown and scepter with cucumber.

Empress

Ingredients & method:
1. Prepare a pair of ½" (1.5 cm) wide slender triangles of the following: green shiso leaf (2" or 5 cm long), squid (3" or 8 cm long) and tuna (3½" or 9 cm long).
2. Prepare 2 pieces of thin omelet cut into an isosceles triangle (the oblique side: 3" or 8 cm).
3. Boil a quail egg. Mix 2 oz (60 g) of sushi rice with 1 Tbsp furikake and form it into a triangle rice ball.
4. Paste the strips of the shiso leaf, squid and tuna on the rice ball in this order. This makes a neckband. Wind the thin omelet around the base (photo).

5. Insert a toothpick in the quail egg and fasten it through the body. Make the face and hair with toasted nori and red pickled ginger. Make incisions in cucumber and make a fan.

＊Make the paper lanterns with red sushi rice mixed with oboro (p.25), toasted nori and cucumber. The diamond shaped rice cake is made of red sushi rice and a thick omelet.

SANTA CLAUS SUSHI

Ingredients [6¼″(16 cm) in diameter]:

1 squid body
a bit of kamaboko (crab
   flavored fish paste)
a bit of cucumber
1 salmon roe
1 green shiso leaf
16 oz (450 g) sushi rice (p.6)

Thin omelet:
1 egg
1 egg yolk
1 Tbsp sake
1 tsp salt
1 Tbsp cornstarch
oil for frying

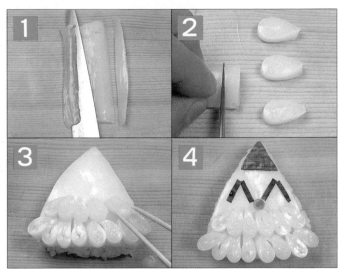

Method: 1. Cook a thin omelet as explained on page 51. Cut into thin strips.

2. Spread strips of omelet all over the bottom of a round mold. Fill 14 oz (400 g) of sushi rice on them evenly. Turn over and take out of the mold.

3. Cut the squid into a triangle with sides 3″ (8 cm) long and a rectangle with sides 1¼″ (3 cm) by 2¾″ (7 cm) long.

4. Cut off the long sides of the rectangle (photo 1). Fold in half and cut into ⅛″ (5 mm) widths (photo 2) and make a beard.

5. Form the remaining sushi rice into a triangle and put the squid triangle on it. Decorate with the beard (photo 3). Make the hat with kamaboko, the eyes with cucumber, and the nose with salmon roe (photo 4).

6. Place a shiso leaf in the center of (2), and put the Santa Claus on it.

SUSHI FOR SPRING

This arrangement was made with the image of rabbits and butterflies playing in a flower bed of tulips. For nigiri-zushi, sea bream of the season and colorful shrimp are used to create a brilliant atmosphere.

Menu suggested for spring sushi:
- Butterfly Roll (p.11)
- Tulip Roll (p.9)
- Shrimp Nigiri-zushi (p.40)
- Sea Bream Nigiri-zushi (p.36)
- Squid Rabbits (p.46)

SUSHI FOR SUMMER

The maki-zushi represents the rose and wisteria which bloom in early summer. The ingredients of the season, abalone and horse mackerel were used for bou-zushi and tuna nigiri-zushi for colorful accentuation of the arrangement. Bamboo leaves were placed on glassware for a cool and refreshing feeling.

Menu suggested for summer sushi:
- Wisteria Roll (p.19)
- Rose Roll (p.8)
- Horse Mackerel Bou-zushi (p.57)
- Abalone Nigiri-zushi (p.39)
- Tuna Nigiri-zushi (p.32)

SUSHI FOR AUTUMN

The combination of the floating chrysanthemum maki-zushi, which suggests the fields and mountains in autumn, and the shellfish nigiri-zushi, which become tasty in late autumn. The earthenware container gives a sedate and warm feeling.

SUSHI FOR WINTER

On a vermilion-lacquered tray the maki-zushi of pine, bamboo and plum were combined. This is an arrangement for the New Year. The sea bream roll and gourd roll are also suitable for festive occasions.

Menu suggested for winter sushi:
- Pine Roll (p.16)
- Bamboo Roll (p.17)
- Plum Roll (p.18)
- Red & White Plum Sushi (p.61)

SUSHI PAINTING
Surprise Everyone with this Playful Sushi
SUNSET-ZUSHI

The scene features a young couple gazing at the sun setting on the horizon of a tropical island. First sushi rice is spread on a platter. The sunset is created from salmon roe, kani-ko (crab eggs), kimi-soboro (grated egg yolk), and yukari (minced salted shiso leaves). The sun is crafted from squid flesh, and toasted sesame seeds suggest a sandy beach. Palm trees, birds and the couple themselves are cut from aspidistra leaves (see p.78). A tuna hibiscus flower graces the lower right corner to complete the island atmosphere.

SOUPS

Generally suimono (clear Japanese soup) is served with sushi, but the simple taste of miso soup is also good. Presented here are some easy soups prepared with seasonal ingredients.

CLEAR SOUP WITH CLAMS

Ingredients (4 servings):

8 clams
1 piece kombu (kelp)
(4″ or 10 cm square)
4 cups water

dash soy sauce
20 kinome leaves (Japanese
pepper plant)
salt

Method: 1. Choose fresh clams which have a good clear sound when they are tapped. Put in lightly salted water to aid in discharging sand. Cut off the hinge so that it opens with ease (photo 1).
2. Put water, kombu and clams in a saucepan over heat. Remove the kombu just before it comes to a boil. Simmer over low heat, skimming off the scum, until the clams open.
3. Pick up the clam with chopsticks, and shake in the liquid to remove the remaining sand (photo 2). Transfer into a bowl.
4. Strain the liquid in a colander lined with cheesecloth and warm. Season with 1 tsp salt and soy sauce, and pour in the bowl. Float the kinome on top.

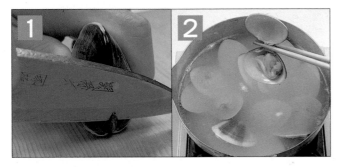

HORSE MACKEREL BALLS IN SOUP

Ingredients (4 servings):

Tsumire (fish ball):
  4 horse mackerel
  a bit of grated mountain
  yam (yama imo)
  1 Tbsp cornstarch

4″(10 cm) naga-negi (leek)
2 green shiso leaves
4 cups dashi stock
4 Tbsp white miso
salt

Method: 1. Cut horse mackerel into fillets as explained on page 34. Chop the flesh into a paste with the knife and transfer to a mortar. Combine with the yam and cornstarch (photo 1) and grind until only some lumps remain.
2. Make the ground flesh into bite-size balls (photo 2) and boil in lightly salted hot water. When cooked and the ball comes up to the surface, remove to a colander and drain.
3. Cut the naga-negi into 2″ (5 cm) lengths and cut into julienne strips (see p.52). Cut the shiso leaves into thin strips. Warm the dashi stock and dissolve the miso.
4. Transfer the tsumire to a bowl and pour in the stock. Add the naga-negi and shiso leaves.

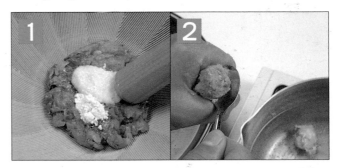

DASHI STOCK

Ingredients (about 4 cups):

2 or 3 pieces kombu (3″ or 8 cm long) /
a handful of dried bonito flakes / 4½
cups water

Method: 1. Remove dirt and sand from the kombu with a wet cloth wrung well. Make some incisions so that it will yield more flavor (photo 1).
2. Soak the kombu in water and allow to stand for about 30 minutes (photo 2).
3. Cook over medium heat and remove just before the water comes to a boil (photo 3).
4. Add bonito flakes (photo 4) and carefully skim off the scum (photo 5).
5. Bring to a boil and immediately turn off the heat. Wait until the flakes sink to the bottom of the pan.
6. Strain in a colander lined with cheesecloth (photo 6).

NEGI & TUNA SOUP

Ingredients (4 servings):

5½ oz (160 g) tuna   Soup:
1 naga-negi (leek)   4 cups dashi stock
1 clove ginger   1 tsp mild soy sauce
                           1 tsp salt

Method: 1. Cut the tuna into bite-size pieces and boil in hot water until cooked. Chop the naga-negi into 1¼″ (3 cm) lengths and boil. Cut the ginger into julienne strips.
2. In a saucepan bring the dashi stock to a boil and add the soy sauce and salt.
3. Put the tuna and naga-negi in a bowl and pour the soup over all. Top with the ginger.

WHITEBAIT & EGG SOUP

Ingredients (4 servings):

3 oz (80 g) whitebait   Soup:
1 egg   4 cups dashi stock
1 Tbsp dashi stock   1 tsp sake
dash salt   1 tsp salt
4 kinome leaves (Japanese   ½ tsp mild soy sauce
    pepper plant)   salt

Method: 1. Beat the egg and mix in the dashi stock and salt.
2. Boil the whitebait in lightly salted water until the color changes. Skim off the scum and pour (1) over, stirring. When the egg has become firm, scoop it with a draining spoon and transfer to a bowl.
3. Bring the dashi stock to a boil in a pot and add the sake, salt and soy sauce.
4. Pour the soup in the bowl and float the kinome on top.

SHRIMP & SHIITAKE SOUP

Ingredients (4 servings):

4 shrimps   Soup:
4 raw shiitake mushrooms   4 cups dashi stock
1 myogatake (a stalk of   ¼ tsp mild soy sauce
    Japanese ginger)   1 tsp salt

Method: 1. Devein the shrimp, parboil and shell. Cut the stem off the shiitake. Make incisions on the cap and boil until soft. Cut the myogatake at an angle into thin slices and put in ice water.
2. In a pot bring the dashi stock to a boil. Add the soy sauce and salt.
3. Put the shrimp and shiitake in a bowl and pour the soup over all. Garnish with myogatake.

MISO SOUP WITH LAVER

Ingredients (4 servings):

4 Tbsp nama-nori (raw laver seaweed)
½ naga-negi (leek)
4 cups dashi stock
3 Tbsp white miso

A simple and easy miso soup. Just put ingredients in a bowl and pour the stock over. The nama-nori contains a little salt, so use less miso than usual.

Method: 1. Rinse the nama-nori in a bamboo colander and drain completely. Cut the naga-negi into thin round slices.

2. In a pot boil the dashi stock and dissolve the miso. Turn off the heat just before the liquid comes to a boil so as not to lose the miso flavor.

3. Put the nama-nori and naga-negi in a bowl and pour the stock over all.

MISO SOUP WITH SHRIMP HEADS

Ingredients (4 servings):

12 shrimp heads
8 stalks mitsuba (honewort)
4 cups water
3 Tbsp white miso

Use the shrimp heads leftover from making sushi. The point is to cook the heads in water to yield the taste. In addition to the shrimp, prawns and crabs may be used in the same fashion.

Method: 1. Put the shrimp heads and water in a pot. When the water comes to a boil, lower the heat and simmer for another 2 or 3 minutes to extract the taste.

2. Dissolve miso and float the mitsuba cut coarsely. Turn off the heat just before the soup comes to a boil and transfer to a bowl.

SAKE-LEES SOUP WITH SALMON & DAIKON

Ingredients (4 servings):

2 fillets lightly salted salmon
4″ (10 cm) daikon
2 scallions
4 cups hot water
3½ oz (100 g) sake-lees
1 tsp salt
1 tsp mirin (sweet cooking sake)

Method: 1. Cut each fillet of salmon into 6 bite-size pieces. Cut the daikon into bite-size pieces and cut off the corners.

2. Put the salmon, daikon and hot water in a pot. Cook over medium heat, skimming off the scum, until the daikon becomes soft.

3. Dissolve the sake-lees. Season with salt and mirin.

4. Add scallions cut into 1¼″ (3 cm) lengths. Bring the soup to a boil to release the alcohol content.

Making use of sushi ingredients
DISHES that go well with SAKE

Prepare dishes suitable for accompanying sake by making use of the leftovers of sushi ingredients, middle flesh with bones of horse mackerel, taenia of scallops and so on. A little thought enables us to enjoy yet one more delicious dish.

HORSE MACKEREL BONE CRACKERS

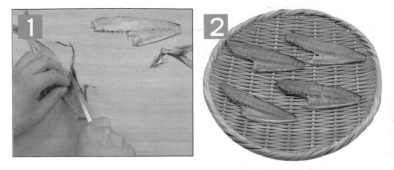

Ingredients (2 servings):

4 to 6 fillets with bones of horse mackerel
1 sudachi (a kind of citrus fruit similar to limes)
a bit of cornstarch
salt
oil for deep-frying

Method: 1. Cut the tail and fin off the fillet (photo 1). Rinse in lightly salted water and remove blood.
2. Arrange the fillets on a bamboo colander (photo 2) and let them dry in an airy room overnight.
3. Sprinkle cornstarch all over the fillets and dust off the extra powder. Heat the oil to 300°F (150°C) and deep-fry slowly for about 10 minutes. When the fillets come up to the surface and the bubbles from bones become scarce, heat the oil to 360°F (180°C) and deep-fry until crisp.

4. Drain completely and then lightly sprinkle with salt and transfer to a platter. Squeeze the sudachi juice over all before eating.

★The point is to deep-fry at low temperature for a long time. Besides the horse mackerel, the bones of conger eel and flounder may be used.

VINEGARED LIVERS OF ABALONE

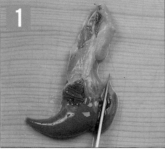

Ingredients (2 servings):

2 livers of abalone
½ cucumber
a bit of lemon
salt

Nihaizu:
2 Tbsp vinegar
1 Tbsp dashi stock (p.71)
1 Tbsp soy sauce

Method: 1. Rinse the livers of abalone in lightly salted water and drain. Cut off the protruding part (which sometimes contains sand) (photo 1).
2. Insert the knife into the liver and open (photo 2). Scrape the sliminess off the other part (photo 3). Cut into bite-size pieces.
3. Rub the cucumber with salt and cut into julienne strips.

4. Put the livers in a bowl and garnish with lemon slices. Combine the ingredients of nihaizu and pour it over all.

★You may blanch the livers in hot water.

OKIZUKE OF SQUID

Ingredients (4 servings):

entrails of 1 squid
Tsukejiru (marinade):
    4 Tbsp soy sauce
    2 Tbsp mirin (sweet
cooking sake)
    2 Tbsp sake
    2 squid bodies
    a bit of negi (leek)

The okizuke of squid is a specialty of Hakodate in Hokkaido. It is a kind of marinade of fresh squid. Presented here is a recipe adapted for home preparation.

Method: 1. Remove the ink sac and thin skin from the entrails (photo 1).
2. Combine the ingredients of tsukejiru and bring to a boil. Let cool.

3. Marinade the entrails in the tsukejiru (photo 2) and keep in the refrigerator for 4 to 5 days until well seasoned.
4. Remove the skin from the body of squid and cut into thin strips 2″ (5 cm) long.
5. Take the entrails from the sack and thoroughly mix with the body. Transfer to a bowl and top with the thin slices of negi.

TUNA SEASONED WITH VINEGAR & MISO

Ingredients (2 servings):

3 oz (80 g) tuna (red flesh)	1½ Tbsp vinegar
2 scallions	1 Tbsp sake
a bit of yuzu (citron) peels	1 Tbsp mirin (sweet
dash salt	cooking sake)
Sumiso (vinegared miso):	1 tsp sugar
2 Tbsp white miso	

Method: 1. Boil the tuna until the color of the surface changes. Cut into bite-size pieces. Boil the scallions in salted water. Remove to a bamboo colander and let cool. Cut the peels of yuzu into julienne strips.
2. Combine the ingredients of sumiso in an earthenware mortar and mix well, grinding. If you want to get rid of the acid taste, transfer the mixture to a small pot and continue stirring over a low heat until steam comes up.
3. Put the tuna and scallions in a bowl and pour the sumiso over all. Garnish with peels of yuzu.

KOBASHIRA MIXED WITH GRATED DAIKON

Ingredients (2 servings):

3½ oz (100 g) kobashira	Aegoromo (dressing):
(adductor muscle in a	3½ oz (100 g) grated
round clam)	daikon
a bit of murame (buds of	1 Tbsp vinegar
shiso)	1 Tbsp sake
salt	dash salt

Method: 1. Put kobashira in a bamboo colander and rinse in salted water.
2. Boil sake to get rid of alcohol content. Drain juice from grated daikon and combine the other ingredients. Mix with kobashira.
3. Put in a bowl and top with murame.

NAMEROO OF HORSE MACKEREL

Ingredients (2 servings):

2 horse mackerel	green shiso leaves
3 scallions	grated ginger
1 Tbsp miso	

Method: 1. Cut the horse mackerel in three fillets and remove the middle bone as explained on page 34. Remove the skin and chop the flesh.
2. Put the miso and minced scallions on the flesh and pound them with the back of a knife until they become a smooth paste.
3. Form it in a circular shape and put on shiso leaves in a bowl. Top with grated ginger. Soy sauce may be poured over if desired.

★You may enjoy it by spreading it thinly and sautéeing.

FRIED SQUID ARMS

Ingredients (2 servings):

2 squid arms   dash salt
a bit of lemon   oil for deep-frying
cornstarch

Method: 1. Remove eyes and mouths from the arms and scrape off the suckers. Cut into 1½″ (4 cm) lengths and wipe dry.
2. Sprinkle with cornstarch and deep-fry in oil (350°F or 175°C). Drain and salt.
3. Put on a plate and garnish with a lemon slice.

BAKED TAENIA OF SCALLOP

Ingredients (2 servings):

himo (taenia) of 4 scallops   Sauce:
2 kinome leaves (Japanese   1 Tbsp tomato ketchup
  pepper plant)   1 Tbsp mayonnaise
                               1 tsp dashi stock (p.71)

Method: 1. Blanch the himo in hot water to get rid of the sliminess. Put in a scallop shell.
2. Combine the ingredients of sauce and pour it over the scallop.
3. Bake in an oven or a grill until lightly colored. Top with the kinome leaves.

★ The shell of a scallop or abalone is used as a container. Wash with a brush to remove dirt and boil in salted water.

YAKITORI-STYLE OCTOPUS

Ingredients (2 servings):

1 octopus arm   Shita-aji (sauce):
1 naga-negi (leek)   2 Tbsp soy sauce
                             2 Tbsp mirin (sweet
                               cooking sake)
                             1 tsp sugar

Method: 1. If possible, use raw octopus. Chop in bite-size pieces. Pour sauce over them and allow to stand for 20 minutes until well seasoned.
2. Cut the naga-negi into 1¼″ (3 cm) lengths and skewer them alternately with octopus.
3. Put on a well heated grill and broil them some distance above a medium heat until colored. If desired, sprinkle with powdered chili pepper or Japanese pepper.

Make Sushi Attractive

CUTTING BAMBOO LEAVES & DECORATIVE CUTTING

CUTTING BAMBOO

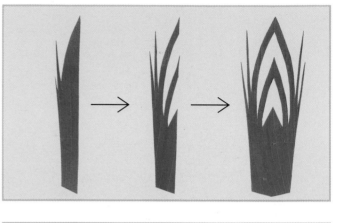

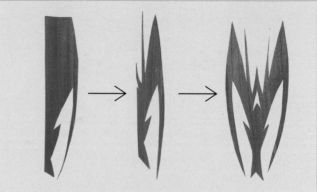

The artistic cuts of bamboo and aspidistra leaves make the color of sushi stand out and, at the same time, prevent the smells of sushi from mingling with each other. There are three kinds of cuts classified by the purposes. Ken-zasa (sword cut) and sekisho (barrier) are set between sushi. Shiki-zasa (carpet) is placed under sushi. Keshoozasa (makeup cut) is used as the decoration. Fold a leaf in half and cut into any form you like with the sharp edge of a knife.

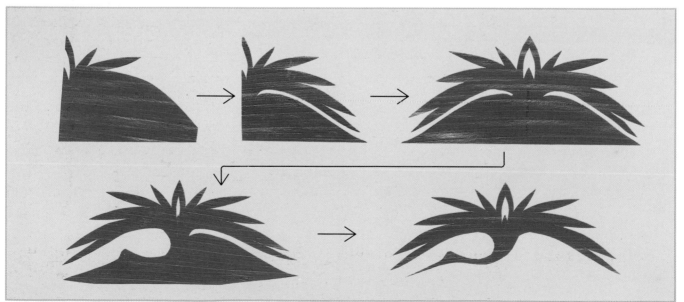

When the sushi is formed to your satisfaction, pay attention to the decoration. If it is accompanied with fancy cut of bamboo leaves and decorative sliced vegetables, the whole looks gorgeous and it will be relished.

DECORATIVE CUTTING

Cucumber Flower

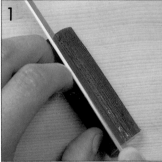

1 Cut cucumber (2¾" or 7 cm long) into half lengthwise. Cut off a small amount of each end. Make 6 incisions.

2 Cut off both corners of the base diagonally. Bend every other stick.

Cucumber Pine

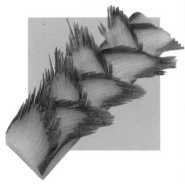

1 Cut cucumber (2¾" or 7 cm long) into half lengthwise. Make small incisions up to ⅓ deep.

2 Cut off the end diagonally. Make an incision aslant by pushing the knife away from you.

3 In the same fashion, make an incision aslant by pulling the knife toward you. Repeat this procedure.

Roll of Takuan

1 Peel thinly all the way around a piece of takuan (yellow pickled daikon) 3" or 8 cm.

2 Sprinkle with toasted sesame seeds and place green shiso leaves and pickled pokeweed (mountain burdock) as shown in the photo.

3 Roll up away from you making the pokeweed the core. Cut into ⅜" (1 cm) widths and skewer two rolls.

Make Sushi Tasty
SWEET-SOUR PICKLED GINGER•
WASABI HORSERADISH•SWEET SOY-SAUCE DRESSING

Sweet-sour Pickled Ginger (Gari)

Ingredients and method (3 to 4 pieces):

1. Pare the ginger and cut into thin slices along the fibers (photo 1).
2. Spread on a bamboo colander and sprinkle with a little salt (photo 2). Allow to stand about 20 to 30 minutes until soft.
3. In a small pot put ½ cup vinegar, 2 Tbsp sugar and ¼ cup water and bring to a boil. Let cool. If desired, add a bit of red food coloring and make them pale pink.
4. Blanch the ginger in hot water (photo 3). Transfer to a bamboo colander and drain. Cool by fanning.
5. Soak in the sweet-vinegar for about a day until well seasoned (photo 4).

Wasabi Horseradish

The particular pungent aroma and pleasingly sharp taste diminishes the smell of fish and accents the flavor. Wasabi perishes from the root end, so choose one which has a thick and not blackish root end. Grate just before using to keep the flavor, wrap the remainder in plastic wrap and keep it in the freezer.

How to grate: **1.** Cut off the stalk (photo 1) and scrape off the rough surface (photo 2).
2. Use a grater with fine abrasive surface like shark skin. Start with the leafy end and move the stalk gently against the grater in a circular motion (photo 3).
3. Pound with a knife to bring out the aroma and pungent taste (photo 4).

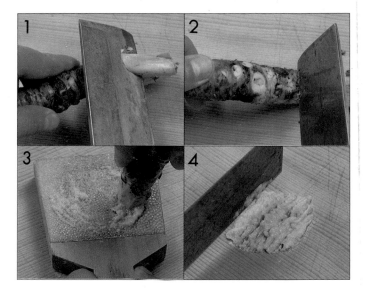

Sweet Soy-sauce Dressing

Dressing made by adding sake and mirin to soy sauce. Boil sake and mirin (each 10% of soy sauce) to disperse alcohol (photo 1). Add soy sauce and turn off the heat just before it comes to a boil (photo 2).